Christ in Your Shoes

Buckner Fanning

Christ in Your Shoes

BROADMAN PRESS / NASHVILLE, TENNESSEE

Contents

Christ in Your Shoes

1. Bread and Bibles

In the spring of 1969, I visited the Baptist Church in Warsaw, Poland, where it was my privilege to worship and bring the Sunday morning message. There I had pointed out to me Mrs. Kamila Michowski. She was asked to stand in the service that morning—90 years of age. She had been ill for a good while, and this was her first Sunday back in church for a number of weeks. Thus she shared a word of testimony, apparently thanking the people for their prayers in her behalf.

The pastor, Mr. Pawlik, who interpreted my message that morning and spoke very beautiful English, told me briefly about this woman. During the German occupation, into a horrible Jewish ghetto where 40,000 people had lived, Hitler pushed half a million Jews. Fifty thousand died within the first month—one of the black pages in human history. This woman, a Christian, jeopardizing her life, would take a Star of David armband, put it on, and go into the Jewish ghetto. Identifying herself with these people in their plight, in their critical hour of need. And she would go smuggling bread and Bibles, always the two—bread and Bibles. She would distribute a loaf of bread and the living bread. Over a hundred people were introduced to faith in Christ because of the bread and the Bibles —the witness, the identification with people in their hour of need—Mrs. Michowski.

There is no crying in the world today heard with more frequency or with greater intensity than the cry for bread. It is not surprising when we realize that while you and I eat lunch today, from the time we have the appetizer until we finish the dessert, 417 people in the world will die of starvation. That's seven deaths every minute, 417 every hour, 10,000 every day, most of them children—crying for bread.

"And when it grew late his disciples came to him and said, 'This is a lonely place and the hour is now late. Send them away to go into the country and villages round about and buy themselves something to eat.' " Send them away.

"But he answered them, 'You give them something to eat.' And they said, 'Shall we go and buy 200 denarii [ten dollars] worth of bread and give it to them to eat?' And he said to them, 'How many loaves have you? Go and see.' And when they had found out they said, 'Five and two fish.' Then he commanded them all to sit down by companies upon the green grass. So they sat down in groups by hundreds and by fifties; and taking the five loaves and the two fish, he looked up to heaven and blessed and broke the loaves and gave them to the disciples to set before the people. And he divided the two fish among them all, and they all ate, and were satisfied. And they took up twelve baskets full of broken pieces and of the fish. And those who ate the loaves were 5,000 men"—no telling how many women and children.

Probably there were 8,000 people—maybe 10,000—in

that crowd that day. This is a fantastic record of a marvelous event. It's interesting that it is the only miracle performed during the earthly ministry of Jesus that is recorded by all four Gospel writers. It made a deep and profound impression upon them. God grant that it will make as deep and profound impression upon us today.

There are many, many lessons to be learned from this miracle at the hands of Jesus. Let me lift from this story a few impressions. First, I am impressed and I am certain you are impressed with the contrasted attitudes. Jesus was filled by compassion (the King James Version says)—filled by compassion. And he said give them something to eat. The disciples said, "We have no money; send them away." Feed them —send them away. Jesus, looking on this great crowd of people, was moved with a deep compassion.

This rushing crowd had completely spoiled the entire purpose of the trip. They fouled up the whole thing. Jesus and his disciples were looking for a period of quietness and retreat, relaxation from the pressing activities of the day. When they got to the retreat area, when they got to the lonely place, it was no longer lonely. It was being trampled down by a milling mob. And it would have been so natural, so very normal to exclaim, with a degree of impatience—"Can't they leave me alone for at least an hour?" But looking at the crowd only one emotion characterized Jesus' heart—compassion. Compassion.

Notice something very significant. The compassion of Jesus Christ was not mere sentiment. It was practical help. It was not just a word of good cheer, as helpful as that can be under certain circumstances. It was not just a word of good cheer— it was a piece of bread. It was not just, "Look up, old fellow"; it was, "Eat up, old fellow."

I think we all need to be reminded occasionally that the Lord sometimes gives not medicine but food. Not medicine but food. In other words he not only heals diseases—he prevents diseases. Too often the gospel is looked upon only as a remedial scheme and too little is it looked upon as a means of maintaining life—maintaining spiritual health, preventing disease, preventing disaster. Surely the Great Physician is capable of practicing some preventive medicine and not always being engaged in trauma room rescue.

Notice the contrasting attitudes—the attitude of Jesus and the attitude of the disciples. When the disciples saw it was getting late and the crowd was tired and hungry, they said, "Send them away so they can get something to eat." In a sense they were saying, "We've had it; these people have had it. They are tired, they are hungry, get rid of them. Let somebody else worry about them, or let them worry about themselves. If they are so ignorant that they didn't come with a day's provisions or if they weren't so infernally lazy they could find bread for themselves—let 'em go. If we feed them, we are only going to be encouraging irresponsibility. Can't do that. If we feed them we are only going to be endowing their laziness. And man —that's horrible. Let them find bread for themselves."

Jesus said, "You feed them. These people are tired and hungry, and you and I must do something about it." Something practical.

There are always people who are aware of the fact that others are in difficulty—we are great diagnosticians. Aware of the fact that people are in trouble, often these are the very people who wish to push off the responsibility either onto the individual himself or to somebody else to handle the problem. Like Pilate of old, they seek to wash their hands in a basin of imagined neutrality.

My state, Texas, faced this problem in a very realistic form in 1969. It voted for increased public assistance for four groups of people—the aged, families with dependent children, the blind, and the permanently and totally disabled. Those four groups. The situation in Texas was then desperately poor. In old age assistance Texas ranked thirty-first, and underline the word *rank*. In aid to permanently and totally disabled, we were forty-third. In aid to the blind, we were thirty-fifth. In aid to families with dependent children, we were forty-fifth. The situation was inexcusable for a state with the wealth that belongs to the State of Texas. Happily, the situation is now somewhat improved.

Public assistance payments in Texas are for those too old, too young, too ill or otherwise too handicapped to support themselves. The average monthly payments to these people are still meager for meeting the basic human needs for food, clothing, and shelter. For many, these payments only make survival possible. Yet there was an emotional reaction against aid to families with dependent children. I didn't hear anybody arguing against old age assistance or aid to the blind or aid to the permanently and totally disabled. But unfortunately, welfare for children! Isn't it interesting how the word "welfare" has been turned into a dirty word in our day? Our forefathers didn't think thus of it, and that's why they incorporated it into the Constitution. But we've turned it into a dirty word.

Now the purpose of aid to families with dependent children is to alleviate the suffering and injuries of poverty and to enable more children to develop into healthy, capable adults. To receive AFDC, a family must be desperately poor. The program helps a family—underline the word family—bring its income up to only $164.00 a month. Before the vote, the amount was $123.00. This is for a family with four or more children—smaller families receive less.

The idea that mothers have additional children to get welfare money is ridiculous. The additional amount doesn't begin to take care of another child. Nor is illegitimacy caused by welfare. Only one in eight illegitimate children in Texas is on the aid to families with dependent children rolls. One out of eight. If welfare caused that one, what caused the other seven?

Nor is welfare utilized to get out of working. Most of the AFDC mothers in Bexar County have little if any education. And the jobs which they could hold would hardly pay for baby sitters unless they were fortunate enough to get their children enrolled in a low cost day-care center, and there's a great shortage of such centers in Bexar County.

In spite of this problem many of the AFDC mothers are working or they are making an effort to find jobs. The April 11, 1969, issue of the *Counselor Reporter* published by the Community Welfare Council of San Antonio reveals these details on families receiving AFDC funds in Bexar County. Forty-three percent were employed; 17 percent are in job training; 15 percent were required at home to care for a husband or a child who was physically or mentally ill; 22 percent were at home caring for preschool age children or were unemployable due to a lack of job skills; 3 percent were employable and were not looking for work—3 percent.

We have been thrilled by landing men on the moon, and I personally have been challenged by it tremendously. It says to me again that America's problem is not a problem of know-how. America's problem is a problem of its attitude, its priorities, its lack of will. And if we can so control the environment that the moon becomes habitable under certain circumstances then certainly we can do the same for Harlem and for the east and west sides of San Antonio and for Appalachia, and for the migrant workers.

You could fill a church with sermons that have been preached from Baptist pulpits on legalized gambling and the control of alcohol in the state of Texas. Let me tell you something. By a thousand to one there is more Scripture in the

Bible pertaining to taking care of the poor and the delinquent and the neglected and the rejected than all the Scriptures combined referring to gambling or to the control of alcohol.

There is another lesson to be learned from Jesus' miracle, and that is the lesson of complementary action. Jesus shows us the proper relationship between the spiritual and the physical. They are inseparable. They are two sides to the same coin.

Notice that Jesus Christ did not make these folks fill out a form. He didn't give them an examination to try to find out—out of all of those thousands of people—which ones were lazy, who was willing to work, or who was moral or immoral by the standards of the day. The need was the call. The need was the call, and he fed a multitude without hesitation or qualification. And anyone reading the New Testament with any understanding at all will recognize quickly the fact that Jesus has obliterated forever the distinction between physical and spiritual. Now notice why I say this.

The multiplication of the loaves and the fishes did not occur in the hands of Jesus. It did *not* occur in *his* hands. It occurred in the hands of the recipients and the distributors. The difference was the fact that he had broken the loaves, implying that they were to be distributed, they were to be shared. He had blessed the loaves. In other words he was putting an ingredient there—the ingredient of selflessness, the ingredient of compassion, the ingredient of concern, the ingredient of love. He was putting an ingredient there that was not there before. After he had broken the loaves, after he had blessed the loaves, there were only five loaves and two fishes. The action was initiated by Christ, but it was continued by man. The disciples distributed the bread to the multitude and the multitude to one another. It was in the distribution, in the sharing, in the giving, that the multiplication occurred.

When will we learn this divine lesson? When will we learn

that it is not by keeping good things that they multiply in our hands? It is when we give them away and turn them into sources of blessing and life and strength and help to others—it is then that the multiplication occurs. It is then that miracles take place.

In the estimation of Jesus something to live on, and something to live for, are inseparable. Jesus Christ gave them something to live on—physical bread—and he gave them something to live for—himself. Jesus emphasized in the conversation which grew out of this miracle that the spiritual food, in the sense that we understand spiritual, eternal food, the spiritual food which he gives is himself. In other words that which Jesus gives us to live on, and for, is himself. It is right, it is as right as Jesus Christ was right, to give physical bread so that men might physically live. And it is right, as right as Jesus Christ is right, it is right to give men spiritual bread so that they might spiritually live. The two are indivisible.

Mrs. Michowski in Warsaw, Poland, learned this lesson a long time ago. Would to God we had learned it. It is not a question of bread or Bibles, it is a question of bread and Bibles.

This teaches me also that I cannot sustain life except by using as food that which has been alive. I cannot sustain life except by using for food that which has been alive. The nutritive properties of the earth and the air must be assimilated for us by living plants and living animals before we can use them. The plants derive life out of the earth. You can live on the plants, but not on soil itself. Cattle find nourishment in the grass. You can live on the cattle but not on the grass. You and I cannot sustain life except by using as food that which has been alive. You and I can make little use of remote, abstract truth. It must be embodied in a living form before we live. It must be embodied in a living loaf and a living person. You see it?

God is remote. God is abstract. It is when the Word becomes flesh, it is when love becomes a loaf of bread, it is when the hidden reason takes human form and steps out on the earth before us—it is then that truth becomes nutritive and God becomes our life. Jesus said the bread which he gives is his flesh which he gives for life. For the life of the world. So Jesus Christ gives us something to live on, and he gives us something to live for, and they are indivisible.

The third and final thought—the concluding act. He told the disciples to gather up the fragments. Now this says a great deal to me. It says something to me about fulfilment. There were twelve disciples, there were twelve basketsfull. Twelve is the Jewish number of completion, of fulfilment. And Jesus is the fulfilment of the Law and the Prophets. It also says something to me about the fact that wealth is no excuse for waste. Never. Fragments of time have made great scholars. Fragments of opportunities seized have saved multitudes of lives. It's also a fact to me, an example to me of the fact that if we will but give our lives he will take them and break them and bless them and use them for the betterment of the world to provide bread and Bibles.

But there is one overwhelming impression that comes to me out of reading this passage of Scripture—it's a new impression, one I'd never seen before. They gathered up the fragments. And who are the fragments? We are. All of us at one time or another have felt very broken and discarded and used. We've sometimes felt there was nothing left for us but the trash heap, and then somebody picked us up.

Eternal truth became a helping hand. He gathered us up. Do you happen to be looking at yourself and asking with the disciples, what are these among so many? What am I in the face of such critical need in the world, only five loaves and two fishes? I'm nothing—fragments, a broken heart, a broken dream, broken plans, broken homes, broken body, broken emotion. God doesn't use anything until it has been broken. You don't get the rainbow until the light's broken. The aroma from the alabaster box didn't fill the room until it was broken. Broken fragments—all of us.

You and I are called in a new and fresh way to give ourselves to be broken, to be blessed, to be used to do two things: to gather up and to be gathered up. This is what Paul meant when he said we save one another. To gather up and to be gathered. Let Christ find you and bring you to himself. And then let him send you into all the world with bread and Bibles.

2. The Strategy of Penetration

We face not only the most desperate but the most challenging hour in the long history of Christendom. Every conscientious Christian I know is seriously endeavoring to determine just what his responsibilities are to Christ, his church, and the world.

The words of George MacLeod express it with disquieting beauty. "I simply argue that the cross be raised again in the center of the market place as well as on the steeple of the church. I am recovering the claim that Jesus was *not* crucified in a cathedral between two candles, but on a cross between two thieves; on the town garbage heap; at a crossroads so cosmopolitan that they had to write His title in Hebrew and in Latin and in Greek (or shall we say in English, in Bantu and in Afrikaans); at the kind of place where cynics talk smut, and thieves curse, and soldiers gamble. Because that is where He died. And that is what He died about. And that is where churchmen should be, and what churchmanship should be about."

How do we know that is where churchmen should be and what churchmanship is to be about? *If* there is any question, then listen again to what Luke records in the fourth chapter. "Then Jesus went to Nazareth where he had been brought up, and on the sabbath day he went as usual to the meeting house. He stood up to read the Scriptures, and was handed the book of the prophet Isaiah. He unrolled the scroll and found the place where it is written: 'The Spirit of the Lord is upon me. He has anointed me to preach the good news to the poor, he has sent me to proclaim liberty to the captives, and recovery of sight to the blind, to set free the oppressed, to announce the year the Lord will save his people!' Jesus rolled up the scroll, gave it back to the attendant and sat down. All the people in the meeting house had their eyes fixed on him" (Luke 4:16-21). It is time you and I fixed our eyes on him and listened very clearly to what he is saying because it has disturbing implications for all of us.

You and I say we believe the gospel, and in a way I'm convinced we do. However, if we do, why is this revolutionary gospel not getting through us to the world? Why is the dynamic of God's love for all mankind apparently short-circuited by the very ones who claim to be his followers? It would be easy to fix the blame on modern culture, technological advance, secularization of society, television or a multitude of other social forces.

Yet most of us know, in moments of agonizing honesty, that the trouble lies within us. We've experimented with every form of evasion known to man. We've tried every gimmick and promoted every program. We've signed all the cards, waved all the banners, tooted all the horns, and manipulated all the members. We've tried everything imaginable to evade the agony of our own calvary, but now the critical decision we face is to die: die to self-love, to pride, to arrogance, to die, and live—or disappear forever in the night of our own denial.

Possibly we are now ready as Christians to hear Paul's words to the church at Ephesus. It is extremely applicable to us. "That is why it is said, wake up sleeper, arise from the dead! And Christ will shine upon you. So pay close attention to how you live. Don't live like ignorant men, but like wise men. Make good use of every opportunity you get, because these are bad days. Don't be fools, then, but try and find out what the Lord wants you to do" (Eph. 5:14-18).

What does the Lord want us to do? Because you and I have the advantage of a written New Testament that was unavailable to the apostle Paul, we can look into the written Word of God and determine with great clarity exactly what it is that he wants us to be and to do. And we find it very clearly. Jesus said, "You are the salt of the earth." He also said, "You are the light of the world." He stated that he had come to cast fire on the earth, and that he had turned over the keys of the kingdom to his followers. He compared his own work to that of bread and water.

Dr. Elton Trueblood helpfully points out, "At first the variety of these figures is bewildering, but a powerful insight comes when we realize suddenly what they have in common. Each figure represents some kind of penetration. The purpose of the salt is to penetrate the meat; the function of light is to penetrate the darkness; the only use of the keys is to penetrate the lock; bread is worthless unless it penetrates the body; water penetrates the hard crust of the earth; fire continues only as it reaches new fuel, and the best way to extinguish it is to contain it."

It is very obvious what God is saying we are to be and to do. Without exception God is saying, through all the figures employed in the New Testament, that the function of the people of Christ is to penetrate the world with the gospel. He is pointing out that the church is never true to itself when it is living for itself because it is then only concerned with saving its own life and the inevitable result will be the losing of its life. If we will only have the courage to hear what the gospel is saying, we will hear it speaking to us in unmistakable terms— reminding us that our primary responsibility is outside our own walls in the redemption of the everyday life of man.

The church must begin to see itself as Christ saw it. Not as a place of retreat from the world, fostering a morbid hatred of life as the evidence of consecration, but a place of Christian acceptance and redeeming love from which people go into every strata of life to live as God's agents—God's representatives—of reconciliation.

I believe that thousands upon thousands of men and women in our churches today are hungry for an opportunity to translate their commitment to Christ into practical deeds of Christian service. And the leaders of the church are largely responsible for their frustrations. We are obligated to God to provide these Christians with means of service through our churches. There they can get their hands on the crucial problems of the world and in so doing share their witness for Christ. These men and women are aware that the New Testament unmistakably teaches that *they* are ministers of Christ in the world of business, homemaking, school, and politics. And the church must provide these men and women with an opportunity to express their commitment to Christ through creative and imaginative ministries of practical involvement. If we fail to do so, increasing numbers of people will ignore the church and, as thousands have already done, find their areas of service through institutions and organizations other than the church of Jesus Christ.

We, at Trinity Baptist Church in San Antonio, are learning exciting ways to serve Christ in addition to teaching in Sunday School, leading in Training Union, or singing in the choir. These are indispensable ministries for equipping and preparing people to witness in the world, yet these are not the only ministries for Christ. There are vast, untouched areas of service where the church can and must begin to prove its concern for Christ by serving our fellowman in his name.

But we have only *begun* to see the church turn from an institution preoccupied with its own survival to a fellowship concerned with being a servant to people in the world. We have only taken the first few trembling steps down the road of genuine Christian involvement, and yet we *have* taken those steps. Whatever has been accomplished was accompanied with great travail of soul. It has not been easy or placid. Yet God has unquestionably honored it, for the life of the church is being renewed and the lives of people outside the church are being reached with the gospel of Christ.

The people of Trinity are sincerely seeking to penetrate the world with the gospel and consequently many new areas of involvement have opened to us. For example, there has been a reorganization and reorientation of our Woman's Missionary Society. We have disbanded the "circles" where the primary emphasis was on studying and have instead organized service groups where the primary emphasis is on personal ministries. Through these service groups the women of the church may minister to a vast variety of needs from work in hospitals and nursing homes to juvenile rehabilitation.

Two of our three local mission churches are situated in some of the most depressed and blighted areas of our community. In these two mission churches we have not only the regular worship services; Sunday School, Training Union, etc., but each church is also an out-patient clinic for the Planned

Parenthood of San Antonio. Many children from these over-crowded, underprivileged conditions—through no fault of their own—find themselves at a disadvantage in their school life and work. Therefore we have begun a preschool pro-gram in mission churches which helps prepare these chil-dren for public school life.

In addition to this, every afternoon after school, there are supervised study halls at our mission churches. In quiet, air-conditioned comfort these young people from overcrowded homes can come do their homework under the supervision of public school teachers from our church who give their time for such a ministry. Reference books and other materials have been purchased to assist them in their studies.

A large percentage of the juvenile delinquents in our com-munity, as in any community, are school dropouts. Therefore, we believe that Christ's ministry should extend to some of the sources and causes of delinquency and not alone to the tragic victims. The Great Physician I believe would approve of some preventative medicine being practiced in his name. A fence at the top of the precipice is as valuable as a hospital at the bottom.

A few years ago we purchased a house to be the headquar-ters for the distribution of food, clothing, and household sup-plies for individuals in need—whether in San Antonio or around the world. We call this Benevolence House. Each year we assist seven churches in Jamaica, where last year 3,000 lbs. of clothing were sent. Also, over twenty laymen from our church spent a week of their own time and at their own ex-pense, living and working with other laymen in these churches in Jamaica. They endeavored to share with them the excite-ment of the gospel message that "every man is a minister for Christ."

Food, clothing and supplies are also provided for students

at the Mexican Baptist Bible Institute, the Mexican Baptist Children's Home, the Buckner Benevolence Maternity Home, the State Mental Hospital, the Tuberculosis Hospital, the Children's Shelter, and the American Cancer Society. Local victims of fire, flood, accidents and illness, were all ministered to in the name of Christ through the concern of Benevolence House. Food, clothing, shoes, bedding, furniture and school supplies were all given as a conscientious response on the part of the people of our church in their endeavor to translate into twentieth-century items the cup of cold water. It is all done in Christ's name and for the glory of God!

Legal help, job placement, location of children in foster homes is also another ministry of compassion for the total needs of men.

Trinity church has begun a ministry to women alcoholics in San Antonio. In our city of three-quarters of a million people there was no place for a woman alcoholic to go but to jail or to the street—no place to assist in the rehabilitation of women alcoholics. In the first three years of operation 190 women have been served and helped back to spiritual, mental and physical health through the ministry of Christ in Alpha Home. Our service consists of providing a clean, homelike atmosphere, spiritual and psychological counseling, AA meetings, job placement, worship with our church in its regular services, and devotional services within the home.

Of the first 190 women, 96 have returned to life and are now gainfully employed and are living useful, effective lives. Life changing commitments to Christ have been made, and women have been baptized into the fellowship of our church. Alpha Home says, "we love you for Jesus' sake." Homes have been reunited, children returned to parents, and lives have been saved. Statistical information is never an adequate measure of the success or failure of any effort, but our statistics are

persuasive to demonstrate that people with this serious problem can be healed and made whole by the gospel of Jesus
Christ.

The County Children's Home in our county had to be
closed for lack of funds so our church has assumed responsibility for its operation. This home provides shelter, food,
schooling, recreation, counselling and spiritual guidance for
dozens of dependent, neglected, and delinquent children.

What am I saying by all of this? The people in our church
have become involved as Christians on a personal level in all
the activities of our community. They have done so because
they believe when Jesus told his disciples to go into all the
world that he meant exactly that. He meant that we were to go
into all the world intensively as well as extensively. He meant
that we were to go "into" and not merely "to" the world. The
world into which we are to go is not just the world geographically, but the world personally as well. We are to go into all
our world—the world of business and labor, the world of sickness and sorrow, the world of politics and poverty, the world
of family and children. We are to go everywhere, to everyone,
in every condition—we are to become "all things to all men."
By "all means"—that is by every possible means—some may
be helped and healed and saved.

And we are thrilled to discover that in response to these
various means, in response to this variety of ministries, some
are being saved! Also, we are excited to realize in Christ, the
liberty to love what God loved—the world; the liberty to serve
what God served—people; the liberty to give what God gave
—life. We are discovering the exciting, frightening experience
of becoming God's agents of reconciliation.

Such reconciling and redeeming involvement has never
been easy or simple. But, I am deeply convinced, that unless
we Christians become Christ's body in the twentieth century;

unless we do in our day, motivated by his spirit, what he did in his day; unless our churches become places of worship where people of all races and classes meet together in Christ through worship and fellowship; unless we become great springs of new life flowing out from our sanctuaries into the hot, parched prairies of human need; unless the churches of America experience a change of attitude and a change in direction, then we will all pass into the graveyard of religious institutions who have lost their lives while trying to save them. And over the doors of our churches and across the entrance to our denominations you can write, Ichabod, "For the glory is departed" (1 Sam. 4:21).

But, wait a moment, I have great hope for the church. I believe that God has committed into our hands the agonizing responsibility of leadership. I believe that we have within many of our churches the seeds of renewal. John Calvin was correct when he said that the history of the church is the story of many resurrections, and I believe that we are on the threshold of resurrection. However, there cannot be resurrection without death, glory without Gethsemane, or the Promised Land without the dusty journey of faith across the desert!

What would happen if millions of American Christians decided to share the truth in faith, to live the truth in hope, and to speak the truth in love? What would happen if pastors decided to become the shepherd of the flock rather than the pet lamb? Some might lose their jobs, many would lose their status, and we would all lose ourselves.

But in the losing we would find our souls. We would find that the gospel we have preached to others could save us from our fears. In moments of painful honesty, we know that many of us are grandstand quarterbacks. We have never really gotten into the game, and yet we are proud of the fact that we have no injuries. We rarely push our boats out into the deep where people are struggling and drowning, and we confuse our cowardly waiting on the beach with having overcome the storm. We have the false security of lifeguards who stand on the bank yelling instructions to a world that does not know how to swim, but we never leave the shore, and thereby lose our souls by not wading in.

What would happen if you and I decided to wade in over our heads? What would happen if we decided to be God's men whatever the cost to ourselves, our churches, our denomination? What would happen if we confessed that we worship at the shrine of numerical increase and financial growth? What would happen if we confessed that racial bigotry and ecclesiastical exclusivism and negative morality have characterized many of us? What would happen if we took the towel of genuine humility and washed the dirty feet of a tired world? What would happen if we became the "servants" instead of the "served"?

I believe a God-breathed spirit of renewal would sweep through the weary life of the American church, and we would become what many think we already are—the people of God. And in the strength of the Lord, we would claim the promise of God that he has "not given us the spirit of fear; but of power, and of love, and of a sound mind" (2 Tim. 1:7). And in the "all power" of the resurrected Christ we could go into all the world and make disciples of all nations knowing that he is with us "even unto the end of the world."

My son Stephen, when he was about seven years old, walked two blocks from our house to the drive-in grocery one afternoon to purchase some candy. On the way, a large German shepherd dog came out to investigate Stephen, and it frightened him nearly to death. The appearance of this German shepherd was the epitome of terror to young Steve. After returning home he related the incident to us, and I asked him what he did. He said, "I just walked along, looking up, praying all the time that God would help me." He then paused a moment and said, "Daddy, if Jesus hadn't 'rosen up' from the grave we'd be scared all the time, wouldn't we?"

I do not know the German shepherds in your life. I know some of them in mine. I know some of my fears—some of my concerns about success, and my fears of failure. I am certain there are many more. But young Stephen spoke the message that I needed to hear and a message that I believe you and I as Christians need to hear in this day of fear and frustration. "If Jesus hadn't 'rosen up' from the grave we'd be scared all the time, wouldn't we?" But you and I believe he *has* "rosen up" from the grave, and in the strength and assurance of this fact, we can go out into all the world to be God's men! Let's go. "For God hath not given us the spirit of fear; but of power, and of love, and of a sound mind" (2 Tim. 1:7).

3. Sign Seekers

In Mark 8:11, we read, "Some Pharisees came up and started to argue with Jesus. They wanted to trap him. So they asked him to perform a miracle to show God's approval. Jesus gave a deep groan and said, 'Why do the people of this day ask for a miracle? No, I tell you. No such proof will be given this people.' With this he left them, got back into the boat, and started across to the other side of the lake."

Matthew 16:1-4 gives further amplification to the same emphasis. "Some Pharisees and Sadducees came to Jesus. They wanted to trap him, so they asked him to perform a miracle for them to show God's approval. But Jesus answered, 'When the sun is setting you say, we are going to have fine weather because the sky is red. And early in the morning you say it is going to rain because the sky is red and dark. You can predict the weather by looking at the sky, but you cannot interpret the signs concerning these times. How evil and godless are the people of this day! You ask me for a miracle? No! The only miracle you will be given is the miracle of Jonah.' So he left them and went away."

This is extremely surprising, particularly because this incident, as recorded in Matthew's Gospel, follows immediately on the heels of the feeding of the four thousand. Equally remarkable is the fact that the Pharisees and the Sadducees united in their hostilities and opposition to Jesus. Hostility, like necessity, makes strange bedfellows. These two groups, the Pharisees and the Sadducees, stood for beliefs that were diametrically opposed.

You would be hard pressed to find two groups of people, two sets or parties who were more different. Yet they came together in their envenomed desire to eliminate Jesus. The question naturally arises, "Why did the religious leaders of Jesus' day have such a reaction?" Why do any individuals at any time in history have this desire for authentication by the abnormal, the extraordinary, the stupendous? What are the causes of sign seeking?

First of all, there is that innate tendency within nearly every man to avoid the anguish of faith and the peril of risk. We want something sure. We don't want any risk involved, we do not want anything unpredictable, we want it all packaged and delivered. We not only do not want to stretch the muscles of our minds, we do not want to stretch the muscles of our spirit. We want to walk by sight and not by faith. Lord show us, show us. It could be particularly difficult for these Pharisees and to some degree, the Sadducees, because they were supposed to be leaders, and a leader is supposed to always have an answer. For these men to admit an inability would be an experience too humbling for them to take. To live by faith would be asking too much.

Most of us want to see the entire journey before we begin, don't we? I've spent a good bit of time in premarital counseling, and I remember one of these sessions with one couple a long time ago. After we had finished talking, I finally said, "Do you have anything that we should discuss, or any question you want to ask, or anything I can help you with?" I could tell by the look on the prospective groom's face that he had a question that his fiancée knew because they looked at each other out of the corner of their eyes, and smiled, sort of embarrassed.

So I said, "It's all right." And he said, "Man, how can I know that this is going to work?" I said, "You can't. A marriage license is kind of like a fishing license. It doesn't guarantee success; it just legalizes the try. In marriage, as in any meaningful personal relationship, in friendship, certainly in the Christian religion, it takes faith and trust. A degree of risk is involved because if there is no faith, there is no trust. If you can see it all before you begin, you can walk by sight and you need no faith."

What if when you started home in your automobile you said to yourself, "Well, I can't see my house from here. I don't know that my house is there. I'm not sure that when I go where I think my house is that there'll be a place there called home. I can't see it."

If you had that attitude you'd spend the rest of your life sitting wondering why you never got home. What do you do? Do you turn on your light and start? You'll *believe* that your home is there. It was there when you left, but you don't know that it's there right now. You don't *know* that it is. You *believe* that it is, and you believe it enough that you'll turn on your lights and start the car.

And when you turn on those lights, you're going to be able

to see a few hundred feet down the street in front of you. You're not going to be able to see all the way to your home. And you'll start driving, and when you get to where your lights were reaching, you'll have some more light, and you'll get home progressively, step by step. You don't see home before you start. You have no guarantee that it's there, and you don't leapfrog from here to there.

You get there by faith, by walking in the light as he is in the light. Detours may of necessity be taken on occasion. Adventures, right! But most of our strongly adventurous kind of life and risky kind of living frightens the daylights out of us. We want a surefire thing, without any question.

This is true in nearly every area of life. Most of us want to be intelligent, but we're not willing to pay the price necessary to achieve it. Most of us want to be physically strong, but we're not really willing to undergo the anguish of exercise to get there. We want it but not really enough to pay the price of getting it. The same is true religiously.

The vast majority of us want glory without Gethsemane. We want resurrection without crucifixion. We want Easter without Friday. Therefore, one cause for the sign seeking attitude is the innate desire to avoid any kind of mental or spiritual anguish or discomfort.

The second error of the sign seeker is a misunderstanding regarding the nature of proof. Man cannot prove God's existence any more than God can. Such attempts would require an infallible third party to act as the judge of God. God himself must be the ultimate judge, if he is to be God.

If you and I require some kind of proof for our belief in God, then we believe or we place our trust, our faith, not in God but in the sign, in the proof. And that sign or proof becomes our God and in the process it becomes an idol, and we become idol worshipers. It's impossible for a third party to be infallible enough that he can authenticate God. What higher authentication can you get for God than God himself? What's the proof that a beefsteak is good? The proof is in the eating.

You can look at that beefsteak all day long, somebody can tell you beefsteak is the most delicious food in the world and you can sit there looking at that beefsteak and saying, "Oh, it just looks so wonderful and smells so good, but how do I know I will like it? How do I know it is good? How do I know it will be good for me?" Well, eat it. "Oh, you've got to prove to me that it's good. Convince me that it is good, and I will eat it. What proof do you have the beefsteak is good?" You eat it. The proof is in the doing.

Jesus speaks about doing the truth in John 3:23. Truth is experienced only in the doing. Jesus healed the man who had a withered hand in the synagogue in Capernaum on the sabbath day. Jesus said to the man, "Stretch forth thy hand." Well, that was the one thing the man couldn't do. His hand was withered. Jesus said, "Stretch forth thy hand," and in the response to the word of God, in the doing of the truth came healing. This is the authentication. This is the validation. This is the proof—the doing!

The third error of this tendency to seek a sign or a proof is the childish and even pagan tendency of many of us to look for God only in the abnormal. Jews of Jesus' day expected the Messiah to come in some pretentious manner, to jump down off the pinnacle of the temple, to come with some great display of power and might. Most of us, even today, judge the degree of God's involvement solely on the basis of numerical response.

When we begin to look at the business meeting reports of the church, what do we look to as the indications of the work of God? Size, numbers, and money. Size becomes our proof. Numerical indications become the authentication of our belief in the spirit of God at work. We wouldn't have seen much in Jesus. He didn't have very much size about him, he didn't have many followers, he didn't have much money, and he didn't exert much influence. More people were converted on the day of Pentecost than Jesus enlisted in the three years of his ministry. What kind of response is that?

How do you judge the degree of God's involvement in the cause? The size? You sign seeker. If it's big, God's got to be in it—not the character of God himself or the character of the work being accomplished. Size is mere numbers and money.

One indication of the spiritually mature person is the capacity to see divinity everywhere. He does not make a great deal of sacred places—if he makes anything of them at all. But he recognizes that God sanctifies all of life, that God sanctifies the common places.

Elizabeth Barrett Browning said, "Earth's crammed with heaven. And every common bush is afire with God. But only he who sees takes off his shoes. The rest stand round and pluck blackberries."

The tragedy of the sign seeker is that he's never satisfied. And the reasons are obvious. For one thing, the desire for a sign is unwholesome in its source. This "show me" attitude precludes any manifestation or revelation of God to the person. Open receptivity and sensitivity are necessary to hearing the voice of God.

Why, a person has only to read the New Testament casually to notice the quite persistent rejection of sensationalism for the sake of the show itself. Repeatedly Jesus repudiated that, resisted that temptation. He rejected it at every turn in his ministry. You see it particularly in the temptations in the wilderness, as he fed the five thousand, even when he was on the cross. "Perform a miracle, come down from the cross, and we will believe on you." That insidious temptation—present at almost every turn in the road—was resisted by him. His temptation was to resort to sensationalism.

Matthew 11:16 reads: "Now to what can I compare the people of this day? They are like children playing in the market place. One group shouts to the other, 'We played wedding music for you but you would not dance. We sang funeral songs but you would not cry, John came and he fasted and drank no wine and everyone said, 'He is a madman.' The Son of man came and he ate and drank and everyone said, 'Look at this man. He is a glutton and a wine drinker and is a friend of tax collectors and outcasts.' "

God's wisdom, however, is shown to be true by its results. I hear people saying, "If you don't act a certain way then we're not going to respond, we're not going to believe. God, if you don't reveal yourself in a certain way and in a certain place, if you do not reveal it my way, then don't come. Do it here, perform a miracle. Prove I'm right. Prove that my faith is authentic." What a sad insecurity that reveals. Sad, sick insecurity.

The faith of some individuals is not based upon faith at all. It is based upon names or things or a creed or people rather than on the character of almighty God himself. In this, we are talking about the character and the person of Jesus Christ. The gospel is its own authentication. Now what is the gospel? It is good news about God. Now let me ask you a question.

Is it primarily a message, or is it primarily a man? Matthew's account of this incident reveals the truth, the answer to that question. Matthew, quoting Jesus, said, "The only sign that they would see would be the sign of Jonah." Now what is the sign of Jonah?

Jonah was the prophet who converted the people of Nineveh, turned them to God. The people of Nineveh repented. The sign which turned the people of Nineveh to God was *not* the fact that Jonah was swallowed by a great fish. They didn't know anything about this, and Jonah never used this experience as a means of appeal. The power of Jonah was Jonah himself. God's man—sharing God's truth. It was this emergence of a man, the prophet with the message of God which led them to a place of repentant faith. It was Jonah, the sign of Jonah was the man, the person.

Now what Jesus is saying here is that God's sign is Jesus himself. It is as if he were saying to them, "It is in me you are confronted with God and with the truth of God. What more could you possibly need? Are you so blind that you cannot see?" There's a truth here and a warning.

The truth: Jesus Christ is God's last word. God has nothing more to say in the sense of revelation. There's nothing more that can be said. That is his last word. Here he is. The manifestation of God himself. Beyond Jesus Christ the revelation of God cannot go. He is the ultimate. He is the final word.

Here is God's plan plain for every man to see. Here is God's sign, the man. And the warning is this: if Jesus cannot appeal to man, then nothing can. If Jesus cannot convince man, no one can. If men cannot see God in Jesus, they cannot see God anywhere in anybody or in anything. So when we are confronted with Jesus Christ, we are confronted with God's final word. We are confronted with God's ultimate appeal in him, in the man Christ Jesus.

And if this is so, what can be left for the man who throws away that last chance and refuses to listen to that last word and who rejects that last appeal? What can be said? Nothing. Nothing. And because nothing more can be said, nothing more can be revealed.

You read some of the saddest words recorded anywhere in any literature in the last sentence of Matthew 16:4: "So he left them and went away." He left them and went away. To die. To die. You reject that, and there's nothing to do but die.

4. Believing Enough to Begin

About six years ago, a young businessman came to my office. I'd seen him in the church services, but I had not met him personally.

He said, "Buckner, I don't believe about ninety percent of what you preach. I've gone to church most of my life, and I can't take it. I don't believe in miracles, I don't believe the virgin birth." He said, "Logic tells me that something had to happen, and so I am slightly persuaded that the resurrection was a fact. I don't think that you can rationally explain the transformation and the attitude of those early followers apart from the resurrection. But I can't take the rest of it. I don't believe the rest of it."

"But," he said, "I've got something down inside of me that keeps crying out. I need something. And if what you've been saying every Sunday is true, you must think I need what you're talking about. I'm going to try it, if you'll let me. I'd like to become a member of this congregation. How much do I have to believe to start?"

I'd never been asked that before. What would you say? How much do I have to believe to begin? I said, "Friend, I think you have to believe enough to begin. Start."

He answered, "Well, I don't believe in the virgin birth." So —neither did I when I became a Christian. Did you? If you were converted before the age of twelve, I doubt if you believed in the virgin birth. I didn't know about the processes of procreation at all, let alone the virgin birth. When I became a follower of Jesus Christ, I simply started. And subsequently I saw that the miraculous story recorded by the Gospel writer, Luke, fits the picture. Then, I believed it; but it had not originally been part of the deal. The invitation was, "Start. Come on, follow me."

You and I have to resist the temptation to superimpose upon those who are just beginning an accumulation of theology that we may have picked up over the twenty or thirty years of our own personal pilgrimage. Have you ever read slowly the account of James and John and Andrew when they first met Jesus? Read it slowly sometime without preconceptions. John the Baptist announces, "Behold the Lamb of God, which taketh away the sin of the world." Here's somebody, I'm not even worthy to touch his shoes. He must increase, I must decrease. James and John and Andrew, who had been following and listening to John the Baptist immediately had their attraction transferred to this carpenter from Nazareth.

And so they come up to Jesus and try to start a conversation. They don't know exactly how to begin, but they're captivated by this personality. They're attracted by this announcement, so they kind of kick the sand with their sandals and stand there a minute, and look off in the distance and look at him. He's looking at them with those understanding eyes, and they say, "Hmm, where do you live?" "Where are you from?"

Did he answer them directly? He didn't say Nazareth or Bethlehem. What if he had launched into a long prepared dissertation on his preincarnate existence in the councils of Almighty God? What if he had said then what one of those men standing there later said about him: "In the beginning was the Word, and the Word was with God, and the Word was God . . . All things were made by him; and without him was not anything made that was made." What if he had said that of himself at that very moment?

You know what those three men would have done? They would have said, "OEEE." They would have drifted away. What did he say? Come on. Start. Come and see. Begin. This is a pilgrimage you're invited to. This is a relationship, not just a status. It's not a contract, it's a covenant. It's a friendship, it's a comradeship. It's a walking down the road together. It's a discussion, it's a disagreement, it's a question, it's a perplexity, it's a hallelujah chorus, it's an upper room, it's a Gethsemane, it's a night of shadows, it's an empty tomb, it's a mountain top, it's a commission, it's a going, it's a becoming. Start.

They came to Jericho. A blind man named Bartimaeus, the son of Timaeus was waiting as Jesus was leaving with his disciples and the large crowd. This fellow was so inconsequential and so unimportant in the scheme of things that they didn't even give him a first name. Bartimaeus, that means "son of Timaeus." Blind man. Unimportant. Disinherited. Not in the establishment. Nothing to offer. Relegated to the sidelines. Second-rater. Son of Timaeus, sitting and begging by the road. When he heard that it was Jesus of Nazareth, he began to shout: "Jesus, son of David, have mercy on me."

And then the crowd scolded him and told him, "Look,

you're upsetting protocol. What do you have to offer, blind beggar? No namer, nameless, faceless? Shut up. You're upsetting things, crying out on the streets like this. We're trying to impress this visitor. He's brought a lot of people here. This is good for local business. These people are going to stay in our motels and hotels and eat in our restaurants and may spend some money. Be quiet. We don't want people like you fouling up things, Bartimaeus."

But he shouted even more loudly. "Son of David, have mercy on me." Jesus stopped. Let me mention something. Those of you who like to preach or want to preach or occasionally lapse into preaching, try that topic sometime. Jesus stopped. What stopped him in his tracks? He is the personification of motion. He, by whom all things were made. He, who set these planets in motion, from whose fingertips dripped the stars, by whose hands our bodies were made, and into whom he breathed the breath of life, so we became living souls. The personification and epitome of all motion, stopped dead in his tracks, while the poor, dirty, insignificant, disinherited, blind, no first-name beggar called his name.

Jesus stopped. That's good news. All it takes to get the attention of Almighty God is the sincere cry of a seeking heart. Not status or name or position or prominence or anything else that the world judges important, just a plaintive cry of a seeking heart, "Jesus, have mercy on me," and he stops. Would to God the church would stop. And I would stop. And not always be so busy with my own thing that I don't hear that cry.

I must confess that I've found myself more often in the company of the crowd that was telling him to be quiet. How do we get around to the wrong side of things so easily? Jesus stopped and said, "Call him. Get him here. Quit standing in the way and get him here. Quit blocking and open the door.

Quit hindering and help. Quit judging and intercede. Call him, get him here."

So they called the blind man. "Cheer up," they said. We're fickle, aren't we? Man, we're fickle. One minute telling him to be quiet and the next minute telling him to cheer up. Just can't quite decide whose side we're on, can we? "Cheer up," they said. "Get up, he's calling you." He threw off his cloak, jumped up and came to Jesus. "What do you want me to do for you?" Jesus asked him. "I want to see." "Go," Jesus told him. "Your faith has made you well."

What kind of faith? Faith enough to cry out. Faith enough to be persistent in the face of opposition. Faith enough to be honest. "I want to see. There are some immediate things that I need. I'm certain there are some eternal things that I ought to want, but right now this blindness looms up before me so that I cannot see around it, or over it, or through it. Oh God, just give me some light. Just for tomorrow. God, frankly I'm not nearly as worried about eternity as I am tomorrow morning. Oh God, help me now." Good, let's start here. Let's begin here. Good, now go. "Your faith has made you well."

Maybe there are others like Bartimaeus. I've been where Bartimaeus was. I was seated beside the road of life, I was blind, I was impervious, I was indifferent, but I was frantic down inside. And I remember the day out of sheer desperation I just cried with Bartimaeus and with Simon Peter as he began to sink beneath the wave, "Lord, save me." And he did. How much do you have to believe to begin? Enough to begin. To start. Ask, you'll receive. Seek, you'll find. Knock once, and it'll open.

About six weeks ago another scripture came to life in my study—a woman by the name of Betty. Her last name is anonymous, she's an alcoholic who resides in a home for women alcoholics that is church sponsored. She came for counseling. She smoked nervously, seemed very afraid, but we talked. Her first recollection of her father, her only recollection of her father, was when he shot and killed her mother. A great beginning for a young life.

Raised by an aunt who nightly went from bar to bar, Betty, at a very early age, was introduced to her aunt's way of life. At fifteen she was hustling. Married three times before she was eighteen. Four children. Two attempts at suicide—alcohol—pills—the whole business. She said, "I have such horrible guilt, for some reason I feel responsible for my own mother's death. I so disrupted the family as I look back on it. I'm sure logically it's not true, but if I feel that way that's it, isn't it?"

She said, "Then, I've got a lot of things in my life to feel guilty for. I'm so afraid to go out and try to meet life without a drink. I'm terrified to even get on the bus and go downtown or to talk to people who are not drinking. I've walked with this crutch for so long that I just don't think that I can walk without it." She said, "This is the first time that I've ever felt like this in my life that I haven't gotten drunk. I've come over here to talk to you instead. What do you have to say?"

Well, I want to confess to you as I confessed to her—that scared the daylights out of me. Inwardly, I cried out, "Oh God, help me to say the right thing." And I promise you that all of your memorized prescriptions and all of your little shallow cliches go out the window. You're talking to somebody that's hanging on the ledge. I said, "Can I tell you about another person that you remind me of?" She said, "I wish you would."

"A Pharisee invited Jesus to have dinner with him." I read her this from the *Good News* version. "Jesus went to his house and sat down to eat. There was a woman in that town who had lived a sinful life. She heard that Jesus was eating in the Pharisee's house, so she brought an alabaster jar full of perfume, and stood behind Jesus, by his feet, crying, wetting his feet with her tears. Then she dried his feet with her hair, kissed them, poured the perfume on them. When the Pharisee who had invited Jesus saw this, he said to himself, "If this man really were a prophet he would know who this woman is who is touching him. He would know what kind of sinful life she leads."

I wonder how he knew. Does it surprise you the Pharisee would know so much about this woman's life? Jesus knew what he was thinking. Jesus spoke up and said to him, "Simon, I have something to tell you."

"Yes, teacher," he said, "tell me."

"There were two men who owed money to a moneylender," Jesus began. "One owed him $500 and the other one $50, and neither one of them could pay him back so he cancelled the debts of both of them. Which one then will love him more?"

"Oh, I suppose," said Simon, "that it would be the one who was forgiven more."

"Your answer is correct," said Jesus. Then he turned to the woman. Now get this picture. He turned to the woman, but said to Simon, "Do you see this woman?" He didn't see her, he saw an image, a reputation, an idea, an impression, the result of gossip or reality, it doesn't make any difference, but he never really looked at her.

How long has it been since you really looked at somebody? Maybe your husband or your wife. How long since you quit pigeonholing folks? Rich, poor, upper, middle, lower class, black, white, yellow, good, bad, religious, irreligious, Baptist, something else. Don't you see, in Jesus there are no more categories? God help us, all the walls are broken down, all the artificial separations are gone.

"See this woman? I came into your house. You gave me no water for my feet, but she has washed my feet with her tears and dried them with her hair. You did not welcome me with a kiss, but she has not stopped kissing my feet since I came. You provided no oil for my head, but she has covered my feet with perfume. I tell you then, the great love she has shown proves that her many sins have been forgiven. Whoever has been forgiven little however, shows only a little love."

Then Jesus said to the woman, "Your sins are forgiven." No qualifications, no question and answer form, no blanks to fill in, no words to say, not a single word had passed between them, not a word. "Your sins are forgiven." The others sitting at the table began to say to themselves, "Who is this, who even forgives sins?" I don't think that was said in sarcasm, I think that was a great hunger manifested. "Who can forgive my sins?" Jesus said to the woman, "Your faith has saved you. Go in peace."

If all of us could hear that one great word—what a difference it would make in our lives. How it would liberate us, how it would bury our anxieties and destroy and vitiate our perplexities. We could stop looking over our shoulder worrying about detection. Thy sins are gone. Thy sins are forgiven. Your sins are forgiven. Accept it. Believe it. Live it out in life. Go in peace. Betty ————, God knows your name, your sins are forgiven. Go in peace. How much do you have to believe? Enough to start!

5. A Street-Corner Prayer Meeting in Moscow

"Ask and you shall receive, seek and you shall find, knock and the door shall be opened unto you. For everyone who asks will receive, and he who seeks will find, and the door will be open to him who knocks" (Matt. 7:7-8).

In Moscow, May Day, 1969, Scott Newell and I were trying to get to the Baptist Church for a five o'clock service. It was a holiday and like any great city in the world on a holiday, or any day for that matter, you have a difficult time getting a taxicab. We couldn't get a taxi at the hotel where we were staying. We tried, we looked, we hailed the cabs as they were driving along the street, but they were all full. There was no discrimination against us because we were Americans. The taxis were not intentionally passing us up and that sort of thing. We just couldn't find a taxicab. We went to another hotel where supposedly there was the location of a permanent taxi stand, but there were no taxis there.

We then went over to Intourist, the tour agency for the Soviet Union. We said to the ladies who were working there—a number of them spoke English—"We have got to get a taxicab." Well, in the Russian equivalent they said with a smile on their faces, "Good luck." Again, no discrimination. They were not making life difficult for us because we were from the West. It was just hard to get a taxicab in Moscow, a city of six-and-a-half million people. It was a holiday, and when they have a holiday, everybody takes a holiday—apparently even some of the taxicab drivers.

We walked out of the Intourist Office, which is located in part of the Metropole Hotel. Immediately across the street from us was a huge statue of Karl Marx, to the right, the Bolshoi Theater, to the left, the Lenin Museum. The Metropole Hotel was the place where the Communist Party before they seized power held some of their meetings. Scott and I stood there on the street corner for a moment and we both lamented. We'd tried to get a taxi, we'd done everything we could to try to get to this church. We had the address. We'd called. We knew they were having a service at five o'clock. And so we agreed that if we were going to make it we were going to need some outside help. And we were going to need the help of the Lord.

Now very frankly I had not prayed for the Lord to help us get a taxi before we needed it, pretty much like the prayer life of most of us. An emergency usually dictates the need for prayer. But it is right to pray in emergencies. And so Scott and I agreed that we were going to ask the Lord for help. And so I walked along there and said to myself, inside of myself, "Lord, now I don't believe you've brought us thousands of miles to spend the evening walking around here on the street. Lord, if you want us in the church service tonight, and I just somehow believe you do, help us to get there."

There were two men standing in front of the hotel. Scott moved on out into the street and started waving at taxis, any car that came along slightly reminiscent of a taxicab. I walked up to the two men standing there. I had the address written down on a piece of paper, and I said, "Gentlemen, could you tell me where this address is? Is it close enough to get there on the bus, or close enough to walk? We'd run, we'd do anything."

We had about fifteen or twenty minutes then until service time, and we'd been looking for over an hour. The man took the piece of paper, looked at it for a few moments and called off the address to the other man. They fell into a conversation about the location of this place. I could tell they were talking to each other about where this was.

That was pretty much what happened there in front of the hotel. These two men were standing there talking, and I was getting kind of impatient, wanting to get the address back and get out there in the street and start waving at the cars again. And I said, sort of in a sense of desperation, "It's a Baptist church."

One of the men looked at me with a look like you have sometime when you see someone you think you know but you can't quite recognize. It was sort of a startled look, a surprised look, a look of semi-recognition as if the light had come. He said, "Come on," and he had the address in his hand. As we left there, I yelled at Scott, "Come on, we've got us a taxi." Well, we went running up there. We jumped into the back seat of this automobile.

I was embarrassed later that we had gotten in the back seat. We started driving, and we'd been driving for four or five blocks when Scott said, "This is no taxicab. There's no meter in this car." We were in this man's private automobile. It took us about ten minutes to get to the church. He pulled up right in front of the church and said, "Here's the address." We said, "What do we owe you?" And he was embarrassed that we'd offer. He said, "Oh, you don't owe me anything." We got out of the car and went into the church. We were there in ample time.

Now, in the course of a number of years, I've had a lot of answers to prayer in my life, just as you have. God sometimes has answered my prayers with yes, he sometimes has answered my prayers with no, he sometimes, most often, has answered my prayers with wait. But never in my life have I had such an immediate, such an instantaneous, such an obvious physical answer to prayer as I had as a result of a prayer meeting on a Moscow street corner. And I've thought about it a lot. It did something to me. It reassured me; and it comforted me.

And with the help of the Lord, I'd like to transfer some of that encouragement and some of that help to your heart. This experience reminded me of some things, some things that I theoretically knew and some things that I honestly believe I believed. But it underlined them. It reasserted them. It put some exclamation marks at the end of some personal affirmations of faith. Among other things it said to me that we're to pray for small things. That our God is a God of little things, of the inconsequentials, the mundane, the everyday.

You know, there've been times when I thought, "I just won't bother God. He's so busy. He's trying to run the universe and keep the world from splitting apart. And we've got war and pestilence and famine and revolution. All of the horses of the Apocalypse are riding through every nation of the world. God doesn't have time to be concerned about whether I have enough bread to eat, or whether I get a taxicab, or whether I make an appointment."

But God's concerned about the most minute aspects of our

life. Nothing's too big for God we say. Oh, that's great. That's marvelous. But nothing's too little for God. And some of us need to start thinking small. I realize that it seems contradictory to a lot of the emphasis of life. But his ways are not our ways, and God is interested in the minutia of life, in the small and the inconsequential, the temporal, the everyday. God is concerned about whether or not you get a taxicab. And the running of the universe does not so preoccupy him that he cannot lead us into the little, the simple, and the everyday aspects of life.

This experience also reminded me of two aspects of effective prayer. Now if you leave either one of these off, your spiritual life is going to be out of balance. And one of these aspects of effective prayer is withdrawal, disengagement. It is introspective, subjective. You can pray anywhere. Oh, it's ideal if you have a closet as Jesus talked about in the New Testament, a place where you can go and shut out the world and pray, but you can do that in a crowd. You can do it on a Moscow street corner, you can do it in an office, you can do it in the classroom, you can do it on a military base, you can do it wherever you are. You can pray anywhere. You can disengage your spirit from the aspects of life which surround you and the whirlwind that beats upon you and you can talk to God. Subjectively, personally. Disengagement is an effective aspect of prayer.

Now this word of caution. Don't dream about praying under ideal conditions. Who gets to pray under ideal conditions? Not even the Lord himself. And the servant is not greater than his master. And it wasn't easy for Jesus to pray or to find times to pray or to find an atmosphere conducive, and it's not going to be easy for you.

So don't say to yourself, "If only I had the time I would pray, if only I had the peace of mind I would pray. If only I could get away from all of the noise and the hustle and bustle of life. Then I could pray." Certainly you and I want to try to create the best possible, most conducive conditions for prayer. That goes without saying. But listen, even if you and I were high in the Alps engulfed in silence, the main obstacle to prayer would still remain. Ourselves. Ourselves and that world of ideas and images and impressions which surges within us for the dominance of our lives.

Let them control you, overcome you, imprison you, and you become their slave. And conditions don't change that. Attitude changes that. Your spirit. I could pray, we could pray, you could pray, on a Moscow street corner and your prayer be heard and your prayer be answered. God could come to you in circumstances, and instead of the circumstances being a hindrance, they could become a means of expression for the answer of God's will. And that which we looked upon as a hindrance becomes a vehicle. That which we saw originally as an obstacle becomes a medium, a means, a mediator of the spirit of God.

You know, this also says something to me about freedom. A word we hear a lot about today. Rightly so. We think a lot about it. The world can take away our external liberties. That can happen. It can happen here. It is happening here. The world can take away external liberties, but as long as you and I don't surrender the citadel of our spirits, our attitudes, our hearts, we are free men. The man who lets himself be fettered has fettered himself. But he who is fettered by force is as free as he was before. His ball and chain become a costume. Freedom.

In Rome, one man in jail, another man on the throne. Nero ruling by chains a prisoner; a man named Paul ruling in chains. Which was the free man? Nero, ruled by his fears and his passions and his hatred? Paul, fast in stocks, chained to a representative of the emperor, but his spirit liberated and free! Ultimate freedom is in the spirit of man, the attitude of man. Within a stone's throw of a statue of Karl Marx who said that religion is the opiate of the people, within a good two iron shot of where we stood was the Bolshoi Theater and the Lenin Museum. And right there in that atmosphere, in that environment, in that place, God gave me the clearest, most physical, most immediate answer to prayer I've ever received in my life.

And this says that wherever you are, however godless the surroundings might be, however antithetical to Christian virtues the atmosphere might be, whether it's an office or a prison, a classroom or a home, wherever it is, God hears you and God cares about you. God will do business with you. And you in your spirit can be spiritually disengaged, you can be spiritually free.

But here's the second aspect of effective prayer. You cannot stay spiritually disengaged. You cannot stay just spiritually free. Prayer must become a part of your life, overtly. You must become physically involved. You must become personally engaged in the world. The second aspect of effective prayer is involvement, engagement, contact, liberation of life as well as freedom of spirit.

Looking at the words of this text we read: "Ask and you shall receive, seek and you shall find, knock and the door will be opened to you." The Lord did not say, "Wait, sit down, fold your hands." Ask and then start looking and start knocking, start searching, start opening doors, start looking for answers. These words are all words of action. Ask, seek, knock. We didn't sit in our hotel room and pray, waiting for somebody to come knock on the door and say, "Do you fellows want to go to church?" That would have been a denial of our petition by our actions however honest and sincere we might have made it.

God can direct a moving object, but he can't do a thing in the world with a stationary, immovable body. And one reason God is not answering some prayers is because people are sitting and waiting with folded hands. However sincere, subjectively, and personally the prayer might be, there comes a time when you are to seek, when you are to get out in the street and start looking for taxicabs. And the answer came in the pursuit of the answer. The answer came as we sought, as we knocked, as we looked, as we searched. Not as we sat and waited, but as we asked and searched.

Now we need to understand prayer as withdrawal, as disengagement, as something subjective, as something intensely personal. But this other is equally important and one reason some of our spiritual lives are out of balance, one reason some of us limp along in life is because we do not utilize the second aspect of effective prayer—engagement, involvement, contact, seeking, knocking, finding.

I have a responsibility not only to meet God with all that I have and am, I have a responsibility to meet the world with all that I have and all that I am. I have a responsibility to give myself to God in totality. I have a corresponding responsibility to give myself away in totality to the world around me. To meet God as we're going somewhere. "As we walked together, our hearts burned within us." Not as we listened to a lecture or listened to a sermon or sat in a prayer meeting. As we walked down a busy thoroughfare we met God, and our hearts burned within us and life became forever different.

Where did Saul of Tarsus meet the Lord? In a prayer meeting? No, he didn't. In a church service? He didn't. On a super highway, on a Damascus road he met Christ. He was driven to Arabia by that experience, but he did not go to Arabia to find God. He found God on the Damascus road. He returned from Arabia deepened from the power of the Spirit, but he met God on an expressway. He met God in life, engagement, involvement, contact. It was there God came to him. There is an inescapable dialectic here. Engagement and withdrawal.

Read the life of Jesus, and you will see this rhythm flowing throughout his life. Withdrawal, involvement. Disengagement, engagement. Mount of Olives, Valley of human need. Out and in. Balance. Dialectic. Withdrawal. Engagement. Now much of my imagined praying is little more than spiritual filibustering unless it produces action, engagement, and involvement in the world.

In Exodus 14, Moses and the children of Israel were on their way out of Egypt when Pharaoh had a change of mind and started following them. They got afraid, and they started complaining. When Pharaoh drew near the children of Israel lifted up their eyes and saw the Egyptians marching after them. And they were afraid, and said to Moses, "Did you bring us out here because there were no graves in Egypt where we could die?" They got angry at Moses.

Moses started talking to God. And God answered Moses. Now notice the answer. "And the Lord said unto Moses, 'Wherefore criest thou unto me?' " Moses, why are you praying? You think God would ever ask that question? He does right here. "Wherefore criest thou unto me." Moses, why are you talking to me? Speak unto the children of Israel. Don't talk to me, Moses. Talk to the children of Israel that they go forward. There's the problem Moses. You don't need to pray any more. You need to act. You know what I would have you do. We've already had that out. Now get up. But "lift thou up thy rod." You do it Moses. I'm not going to. You do it. You lift up thy rod and stretch forth thy hand. Quit talking to me, Moses. Pick that rod up and stretch out your hand. Talk to the children of Israel and divide that Sea and the children of Israel shall go on dry ground through the midst of the sea.

We've prayed long enough! Some need to start teaching a Sunday School class, start visiting, start giving, start going for God. You don't need to pray any more. God interrupts your prayer. Get with it. Do what you already know. Be what you already ought to be. Do what you know you ought to do. Don't come complaining any more. Lift up your hands. Get with it.

In the book of Joshua, the children of Israel got to the Promised Land, and they lost a battle because Achan disobeyed God. The children of Israel just started lamenting and complaining, and Joshua did the same thing. Joshua said, "Alas oh Lord God, wherefore hast thou at all brought this people over Jordan, to deliver us into the hand of the Amorites, to destroy us." Is this why you brought us God? To kill us all? Would to God that we had been content and dwelt on the other side of Jordan. Listen to that. God's man talking like that. And the Lord said unto Joshua, "Get up. Wherefore liest thou upon thy face." What are you praying about Joshua? Get up. "Israel hath sinned." That's the problem Joshua. No use for you to pray as long as you willfully and repeatedly and intentionally keep evil in your heart.

And today we have the same problem. You can come to church and pray all day. You can have counseling with the pastor or others. That's not going to do it. You can read your Bible. You can get on the floor crying to God.

Get up! Clean up your life, get out of here and go to work. That's what God says. And my friend, this is the second aspect of effective prayer, and it's the neglected aspect and the reason a lot of us just limp along. So this is to be the Christian life. We have been disengaged from the problems of life, and now we need to get engaged. We need to get involved. We need to get in contact with the world. We have prayed, confessed, and been cleansed, and it's now time to get up and get out of here and get to work. Start putting into practice that which has taken place spiritually within us.

God is always with us in all of the little, everyday burdens of life. He will hear us, he will lead us, he will be with us provided you start looking for a taxi to get somewhere and do something, be something better because you've been here. If you don't, don't be surprised if your life turns sour or caves in, if you're frustrated or angry or wishing you were back in Egypt or asking God to let you die. If you don't put what Christ gives you into practice, it will become molded manna, and it will contaminate your whole life. Get up and go.

6. Busy Man, You've Had a Little Day

Most of us probably at sometime or another have said or thought, "I have never been so busy in my entire life." Have you said that? Some of you may smile—recalling you have said that. I have; I guess most of us have thought it. I am confident that we are living faster, traveling further, working harder than ever before in our lives. We are always on the go. In fact, a woman said recently, "I've never been so busy in my life, in fact, I feel like I'm just running a taxi." You may have said that.

Now often we speak of activity as if it were intrinsically evil, as though there were something about activity that within itself was wrong. This is unfortunate because it can develop the erroneous idea that the ideal life is one of ordered, uninterrupted idleness. And certainly this is not so. There is no morality in laziness. Idleness and indifference are not the hallmarks of spirituality. There is no sin in work. There is no sin in accomplishment. Quite to the contrary, work is a most noble and needed virtue.

Why then, do so many of us feel so guilty about it? And, apparently, we do feel guilty because we talk about it a great deal. I think we feel guilty about it because we recognize occasionally, that though we are engaged in a great deal of activity, though we are very, very busy, we are still much of the time terribly empty and frustrated.

One reason that we feel this way is that we do not really believe that our activity, our effort, our work has any real significance, or produces any real accomplishment. We get tired. What *do* we accomplish? And this is one reason I think for our hangup. We don't really feel that our activity, our work, our effort, makes any significant contribution to life—that it is really important. We come to the end of a busy day, we close the door to the store of activity and turn off the light in the show windows of our personalities, and take inventory of the day's activities. Often we come up with a great big zero. Busy man, you've had a little day.

Why certainly we would feel differently about this if we believed somehow that our activity and our work had any eternal or even temporal significance about it. If we really believed that we were part of something big, but obviously most of us do not. And many people feel this way and consequently say in one form or another the words of T. S. Eliot, "I have measured out my life with coffee spoons."

When this loss of zest for life, this lack of meaning to life, this lack of enthusiasm for life happens, men inevitably and invariably turn to some substitute—a substitute which they hope will add some significance, some excitement, some meaning, some effervescence to their rather barren, monotonous lives. One such substitute is the frantic pursuit of pleasure.

Another is alcohol. To another it may be the accumulation of more money than they could ever spend in ten lifetimes.

Another escape mechanism, calculated to help man avoid the sense of futility that grips him most of his waking hours, is when a nation tries to avoid a sense of emptiness in life by engaging in death—by engaging in war. In our efforts to build a lasting peace, men and women of goodwill have operated on the assumption that men hate war and want to abolish it. They operate on the fact that the desire of the world is for peace, not war. Yet when the truth of the matter is known we like war better than peace. One reason the world seems to engage in war with such perennial regularity is because in war men escape boredom and mediocrity and dullness; some of them also make a great deal of money.

Life suddenly has meaning and purpose. It is very instructive and very disillusioning to note that in England today there are many men and women who will regularly tell you that they look back to the years 1940 and 1941 with nostalgia. Those were the days in which they really lived. War days. The time of imminent invasion, bombs falling from the sky, but they were part of something big. They stood shoulder to shoulder in a great cause. Thrilling deeds were performed, heroic acts. Great rhetoric sustained them in those hours of darkness. Life had meaning, life had purpose, life had a goal.

Then peace came. The danger was removed. And they fell back into a monotonous regularity. Boredom returned. Do you remember the academy award winning movie made of the book that followed World War II? What was the name of it? About the war. *The Best Years of Our Lives.* War. Tragic.

Let me introduce you to the man in the Bible who typifies this attitude and this problem. You'll meet him in 1 Kings 20:40: "And as thy servant was busy here and there, he was gone." Now that little verse was part of a parable spoken by one of the prophets to King Ahab. This prophet was rebuking King Ahab because of his leniency in dealing with Benhaddad, the King of Syria, whom Ahab had just defeated in a battle.

Listen to this man in this parable confess to his own failure. Listen to this admission from his own lips, "And as the King passed, he cried to the King and said, 'Your servant went out into the midst of battle; and behold a soldier turned and brought a man to me and said, "Keep this man. If by any means he be missing, your life shall be for his life." And as thy servant was busy here and there he was gone.' " Here is the confession from the man's own lips. The dust of battle had settled, the prisoners were being captured, the final operations were taking place, the consolidation of victory was being enacted, and this soldier was given charge of a prisoner.

In my imagination I see him. Try to see him in your imagination. Apparently this prisoner was a most significant military prisoner because the instructions were, "You guard him, you watch him, and if you lose him, we're going to take your life in his place." It was a most important responsibility. I can see this soldier who was instructed to guard this special prisoner, with his head erect and his shoulders back, with a sense of pride on his face because he had been given this significant responsibility.

He had a purpose in life, and he realized the need of watching this prisoner with all diligence and care. Suppose the next day I happened to drop by the guard house to see my friend the guard who is watching his prisoners. I can't find him. A new guard's in his place. I say, "Where's my friend?" He gestures to the cell. "No, I'm looking for the guard who was guarding the prisoners. You mean, my friend's in there? You mean he let the man get away? He did not fulfill his duty, he did not accept his responsibility effectively?"

I said to my friend, "Buddy, what happened to you? He overcame you, that's what it is, wasn't it? Some of his friends came, and they effected his release. They got him out of here, that's what happened, isn't it? He surprised you, he caught you when you weren't looking, that's what happened. You went down fighting though, didn't you? Sure you did."

"No, you really embarrass me to come here and to ask me about it. I wasn't surprised, I wasn't overpowered, a bunch of people didn't jump on me and release him. Great day I don't know what happened! I just got busy, I was busy here, and then I looked up and he was gone."

"Well, I'm sure it was important business you were engaged in, wasn't it? Tell me sir, what were you doing? What was so important that it took precedence over your guarding that prisoner? What was so important that it took precedence over the command of your King? What was it, huh?"

"Well, I don't really know . . . I . . . I can't really be specific about it. . . . I . . . I do know I was busy here and there, I don't remember doing what, but suddenly he, he was gone." Failed. Tragic, dismal failure. Well, I think we have every right to ask the question, Why?

Why, because we may learn a lesson about ourselves in asking the question. Why? Well, there're a number of reasons. First of all it's obvious that this man did not fail because of anything that he did. He didn't commit some terrible crime, but there he is seated in the jail, in the prison in the place of the man who escaped, and his life is going to be taken in exchange for the prisoner's. He's going to die, but he didn't murder anybody. He didn't steal anything, he didn't bear false witness.

This man was a terrible, tragic failure, not because of what he did, but because of what he didn't do. He failed to do what the king had ordered him to do. These sins of omission are so dangerous because they are so subtle. So subtle, because they are less flagrant, because they are less violent, because they are less overt, because they carry with them no social stigma.

We all have the tendency to minimize the tragic consequences in life of the sins of omission. How foolish and how immature are some people who think that a man is a pious Christian simply on the basis of what he does not do. When we will ever grow beyond that infantile concept, God only knows. The Lord tries to tell us this in the Bible time after time after time, but we don't listen or won't listen. It is so much easier to be a rule-obeying legalist than it is to be a person-loving Christian. So much easier.

You remember in the Bible the incident that Christ had with the fig tree? It was during the last week of his life when on the way from Bethany to Jerusalem he saw this fig tree and he judged it. Why did Christ judge that fig tree? Because it had very poisonous figs and was corrupting the earth? No, that wasn't the reason at all. It was bearing no figs at all. That was the cause of the judgement. Not because of what it did but because of what it wasn't doing.

What was the sin of the man we call Dives? That poor man lying at his gate, what was the story Jesus told about him? Did he beat him, did he kick him, did he drive him away, did he curse him? No, he did absolutely nothing. And over that failure to assume responsibility for a human being in need, Dives stumbled into a Christless eternity. Not because of what he did, but what he didn't do, Christ saw him in hell.

What was the sin of the five foolish virgins that Jesus told us about in the New Testament? Did they fill their lamps with

water and thereby make them ineffective? No, they didn't fill
their lamps at all. They did nothing.

What was the charge brought against those in Matthew 25
to whom the judge said, "Depart from me, I never knew you."
What was the charge? What they did? Stealing, lying, adul-
tery, murder? What was it? Listen to it, "Inasmuch as ye did it
not." Did it not. That's the indictment.

The reason that this man in our story failed and failed so
miserably was not because of something he did, it was because
of something he did not do. Let's face it, many of our failures
today stem from the same source, do they not? Many of the
failures of the church can be directly attributed to this attitude. The attitude that says that the church is supposed to be
nothing more than a religious data processing computer,
rather than a warm, living, loving, body of Christ.

Wasn't it Dante who said, "The hottest places in hell are re-
served for those who in an hour of crisis do nothing." "Because you're neither hot nor cold I will spew thee out of my
mouth," says the risen Christ.

The man in our story, therefore, did not fail because he
lacked information or because he was ignorant. He knew very
well what his responsibilities were. They were made extremely
clear, "You take care of that prisoner, you watch him and
guard him, and if you let him get away we're going to take
your life in his place. We want to impress upon you the fact
that you are to watch that prisoner." He knew. He couldn't
plead ignorance at all.

Certainly all of us need to know a great deal more than we
know. But I believe that the greatest need in the world today
among Christians is not for more information, as helpful as information can be.

The greatest need in the moral realm, the greatest need in
the religious realm, the greatest need in the life of the church

today is for the individual Christian and for the collective body of believers to do that which they already know. "If any man willeth to do the will of God he shall know," said Jesus.

In other words, the only way God is going to reveal more of himself is for us to start doing what we already know. Some of you already know what you ought to be doing in regard to your time, your talent, your money, your influence. your utilization of church facilities for Christian ministry to the world. You already know! You need to do what you already know, because Jesus Christ is the only thing you get more of by giving him away, and the only way you get more is to give away what you have.

If you keep trying to collect religious data, if you keep filling notebooks full of religious information, you'll be as dead as the Dead Sea, no life in you and no life around you. Christ comes to be given away, Christ comes to be lived out in the arena of everyday contact. To do the will of God is the supreme accomplishment in everyday life. Not to know it, to do it. For the knowing of it comes in the doing of it.

You don't need more information, we need a great deal more inspiration, to do that which we already know, to exercise the muscles we already have, to employ the resources that are already given to us. Theological knowledge and spiritual maturity are not identical. If they were the devil would be the world's greatest Christian. A man does not mature as a Christian on the basis of accumulated religious data. A man matures as a Christian on the basis of obedience. "Why do you call me Lord, Lord, and do not the things which I say?"

One explanation for a great deal of the spiritual adolescence in the Christian world today is that some people get more interested in what they can learn than in what they can be. Spiritual truth is not intended simply to teach us something. Spiritual truth is intended to *make* us something. The man in our story had adequate information. What he needed is what you and I need—commitment, dedication, consecration, and faithfulness. That was the reason he failed and that's the reason you and I will fail. Not a lack of information; a lack of seriousness about our commitment, and a lack of dedication to the cause.

Something else, this man didn't fail because he lacked ability. Why if he'd gone down fighting, if he had any scars to show for his resistance, we'd have made a hero out of him. The church would have knighted him. The King would have honored him. That wasn't the reason he failed. He didn't fail because he lacked ability.

Not one person will fail because he lacks ability. Does that mean that you and I can do anything we want to do, and everything we want to do? That's foolishness. I could begin right now to study art and for the rest of my life, day and night, without eating and without sleeping, I could study art. I wouldn't be a Michelangelo. Face it, you can't do everything you want to do.

Although you and I can't do everything, we can do infinitely more than we are doing because every one of us can do successfully whatever God has called us to do. Whenever God calls a man, he not only calls that man to a task, but he supplies the effective ability with the call necessary to perform that task whatever it is.

Every man's life is a plan of God, and every man can do whatever God called him to do. If the call is responded to by faith in your heart and life and obedience in your living, it will bring with it the power of accomplishment. Christians do not lack for ability, not individually, not collectively, in the life of their churches. You can do some things that nobody else on the face of the earth can do. There're some things you can do, and if you don't do them, they'll not be done.

I heard about a man recently who spent about an hour and a-half riding around the block downtown trying to find a vacant parking place because he wanted to park on somebody else's nickel. Some people spiritually want to park on somebody else's nickel, on some widow's mite, when they have the ability and should have the commitment to carry their part of the responsibility and shoulder their portion of the burden. I believe every man's life is a plan of God, and God has somethings to do through you. If you do not do it, then it will not be done.

We will not fail because we lack ability. This man didn't. He didn't fail because he was lazy either. He wasn't lazy, he was busy. He was tired all the time. Couldn't remember why he was tired or what he'd been doing, but he was tired. And here's the key to his failure. He failed because he was busy at the wrong things.

One of those unfortunate souls with so much to do, so many engagements to keep, so many functions to attend that he didn't have time to do his primary duty. He didn't have time to be true to himself, to his God, to his own responsibility.

Do you know anybody like that? You do a thousand and one good things, but I cannot help but wonder if you sometimes get so busy here and there that you lose the peace of God in your heart. When you get too busy you neglect the word of God, you neglect your family, you neglect the church, you neglect God's work in the world. Worship becomes a matter of convenience. If your activities cause you to neglect the word of God, if your activities cause you to miss the stairway that leads to the upper room, you're too busy. Busy here and there.

Now, if your life is to be effective, if souls are to escape tragic shipwreck, if we're to live big lives as well as effective lives, then you and I must listen once again to the words of the most sane and most successful man that ever lived. "Seek ye *first* the kingdom of God, and all these other things will be added unto you." If you do, when you come to stand before God he will say to you, "Well done thou good and faithful servant, enter thou into the joy of thy Lord." Busy man, you've had a big day.

7. How to Do What You Don't Want to Do

Much of my time is spent in personal counseling with people who are being forced for one reason or another to do things they don't want to do. For some, it means going to the war in Southeast Asia; for others, it means taking a position of conscientious objection. Some labor at a job they detest, while others can't find a job that will support their needs. The point is that, at one time or another, nearly all of us are faced with the necessity of doing things we don't want to do.

So I would like to share some ideas about things you don't want to do—things we wished we were. not forced by circumstances to do. This applies to the soldier in Vietnam; it applies to the conscientious objector; it applies to you; it applies to me.

You and I may not have to go to the steaming jungles of Southeast Asia or go to jail for our convictions. But we do have to go to work or school. We do have to go to the concrete and asphalt jungles of the city where we work. And we may be imprisoned by circumstances and conditions beyond our control. We may not lose our lives—something worse may happen. We may lose our souls.

I would like you to approach with me a moment in the life of Jesus and approach it very reverently. And that moment is the moment in Gethsemane. The background of this experience was, of course, the Upper Room and the observance of the Passover with his friends—the initiation of the Lord's Supper—a quiet time of fellowship together. As you read about it in the New Testament, you may not be impressed with it any more. It seems to be a very happy gathering of close friends. They ate together; they sang a song together; they went out to Gethsemane.

This account is very difficult to talk about. Christ asked his friends to pray for him. Think of that. Think of God asking you to pray for him. And the English vocabulary does not afford us a word to translate fully—he threw himself on the ground. The violence of it is impossible to communicate. He threw himself on the earth. Crushed.

What a picture! The Creator of the world lying face down in the dust he had made. The Scripture says that he was distressed and he was troubled. This says something to me about my distress and yours. Our trouble is not always the result of our personal sins. It was certainly not in the life of Jesus. All trouble, all distress, all difficulty, all anguish, all lonely nights are not the result of personal sins. Not in the life of Jesus, nor in our lives. And he cries out: "Father, Father, please if there is any other way—please."

Silence.

And he gets up and he's sweating, as it were, great drops of blood, wringing wet, dust sticking to his face. "Simon, Simon.

My God, my friend couldn't you pray with me one hour? Please. Simon, the spirit is willing but the flesh is weak."

I wonder if he was referring to himself—not preaching to Simon but describing himself. "Man, pray with me. Help me. I'm in deep, deep water."

"Father"—he prayed it all over again, the New Testament says, the same prayer. "All right, if it can't pass except I drink it, I drink it. If there's no way through it but to go through it —I'll go."

Silence. Not a word from the Father.

At his baptism—"Thou art my beloved Son." At his transfiguration—"This is my beloved Son." At his Gethsemane— nothing. Silence. His prayers weren't getting any higher than the olive tree, as he saw it. The only sound he heard was the heavy breathing of his sleeping friends, to be followed by the soft hiss of a betrayer's kiss.

After a brief flurry, they all ran. The one who had said, just a few hours earlier, "Though everybody forsakes you, I'll never forsake you. Though I should die, yet will I not deny you." He got in a fight and took off.

Well, is that the end of it? For Jesus? For you, for me? No, because some help came, but it came from three very unexpected and unlikely sources. You see, God's like that. His ways are not our ways. Help came. A word came, but it came from unexpected people in unexpected circumstances.

First was a man by the name of Simon. Isn't it interesting? One Simon left him, but another—Simon of Cyrene—was found. They said, "Hey, you. This Nazarene can't carry his cross—pick it up."

"But . . . but I don't want to."

"I don't care what you want to do—pick it up."

"But you see I've come from miles away to observe the

Passover and if I touch that cross I'll contaminate myself and I'll not be able to . . ."

"Shut up. Pick it up. Pick it up. You're going."

Isn't this a picture? Here's one man forced to do what he did not want to do for another man who was being forced to do something he didn't want to do. Life's like that. Isn't it amazing and marvelous how help so often comes from sources like that? And out of it always comes good when God is in it.

This man had two sons, the Bible tells us. One was named Alexander, the other was named Rufus. The Apostle Paul, later writing to the church at Rome, said to give greetings to Rufus. Most biblical scholars believe that Rufus in the church of Rome was the son of Simon of Cyrene. Apparently, Simon's family became Christians because of an interrupted trip, because of plans that went awry, because of circumstances conspiring, because a man had to do what he didn't want to do—carry a cross.

Jesus didn't want to die. Only a fool wants to die. And have you noticed that even Jesus needs help to carry his cross? No man can do it alone—not even God. Even Jesus needed help to carry his cross. So do you and I.

That's what the church is—a fellowship of cross carriers. And we bear one another's burdens at times. And we help other people with their crosses at times—even when it may interrupt our plans. Even when it may not be what we want to do. Just as we've been helped. Some people have helped us carry our cross.

Here's something else—fascinating.

The eternal God of the ages wrapped up in human flesh, named Jesus Christ, allows himself to be helped. It takes great strength to admit that kind of weakness. This One unto whom had been given all power, all authority, in heaven and in earth, allowed himself to be helped.

You know some of us look great on the surface. And we refuse to admit our humanity. We exclaim often about being sons of God. Seldom do we hear "son of man" from our lips, as we heard it from the lips of Jesus. His favorite term for himself—Son of man. Consequently we lose life's battles often. We try to play God—be our own God. And refuse to be a part of the company of the cross bearers. We try to get it there ourselves, and we don't make it.

H. G. Wells has a fascinating story. I think the title of it is "Ninety-Nine"; I read it years ago. It's about a group of people on board a vessel, a sailing vessel. And down in the hold of the ship, a piece of machinery broke loose. It was in heavy seas, and that piece of machinery was sliding about down in the hold, tearing it apart, threatening the life of the vessel. And everybody on board ship was playing like it wasn't there. Does that describe your life?

Often we look like Titanic souls, singing "Nearer My God to Thee" up on the top deck, when down underneath all hell's breaking loose. And we are about to sink in the cold, dark waters of our own horrible pride. Let yourself be helped. Jesus did. We can.

The women who followed also helped him. When you cannot do anything else, you can sympathize. They did follow, weeping. That's insufficient, if more can be done, but that's certainly preferable to sleeping indifference that characterized the life of his disciples. The women wept. Our capacity to care is being destroyed in our day, isn't it?

Maybe we are doing it to ourselves—maybe we are afraid of caring. Maybe we are afraid of showing any deep feelings because they might get us to Calvary. And things get sticky there.

Finally they got the cross to Golgotha. They nailed him to the cross. I don't suppose we are capable of imagining what went on in the heart and the mind of Jesus. I only know what goes on, to a degree, in my own heart and in my own mind. When you feel forsaken by God, by your friends, by society, suddenly, somebody next to you, in equally bad shape, turns as at Calvary, and says, "I believe in you." Thus Jesus heard it: "Yes sir, I believe in you. You're it. You've got it. And you have something I don't have, so help me. Remember me when you come into your kingdom."

A thief, being crucified with him. "I believe in you." And those words are magic. When you do feel forsaken by God, by man. When the sun has gone out of your sky and the earth shakes beneath your feet, when you feel you are impaled on a cross of circumstances, when the world rolls dice for what you have, suddenly, somebody speaks. And you look to see who it is, and it is One who himself was numbered with the transgressors, one who wanted another way and found that there was no other way if you want ultimate victory, one who drank the cup all the way to the bottom. He speaks to you on your cross, at your Calvary, and he says, "I believe in you. I believe in you. Trust me and let me help you. I know how you feel, I've been there. Man, I've been there. Trust me. And I'll bring you through this. Believe in me. And I'll make you to be more than conquerors. Trust me. And all victory will be yours."

The sun comes up again, and the lights come on again in your world. Resurrection is certain, victory is guaranteed, and you, even in the midst of your Calvary can exclaim with him who speaks to us thusly and say, "Father into thy hands I commend my spirit." And there, sir, is life.

8. How to Love Someone You Don't Like

I once made a statement about the fact that we need to have our spirits changed, our attitudes changed. And a very fine lady in our church, speaking with her husband said, "That's true, but how?" A militant in a civic meeting I attended said, "What is needed in this community is an attitudinal change." Right—true—agreed—amen! But how?

In Mark 12, Jesus had a remarkable experience. He is assailed and questioned by a variety of groups all attempting to discredit him. "The Jewish leaders tried to arrest Jesus" (Mark 12:12). Now this attempted arrest was on the basis of a parable that he had told which they thought reflected upon them. They did have the intelligence to see themselves in the parable, which is commendable. But their reaction was one of hate, and they tried to arrest Jesus.

Some Pharisees and some members of Herod's party, Herodians, were sent to Jesus to trap him with questions. Some Sadducees came to Jesus, and a teacher of the law was there who heard the discussion. He saw that Jesus had given the Sadducees a good answer so he came to him with a question. "Which commandment is the most important of all?"

"This is the most important one," said Jesus. "Hear Israel, the Lord our God is the only Lord. You must love the Lord your God with all your heart, with all your soul and with all your mind and with all your strength. The second most important commandment is this: You must love your neighbor as yourself. There is no other commandment more important than these two."

Now I do not believe that in this passage of scripture Jesus Christ is merely giving us some advice. However sage and impressive it might be, Jesus Christ is not just telling us what to do—not merely counseling. He is giving an explanation of his own attitude and his own actions. He is showing his own spirit despite this cauldron of hostility which had been precipitated by these hostile groups coming to him, trying to arrest him, trying to trap him. He is explaining in words what they had already seen and were seeing lived in the word of his life.

What is he saying? How can you and I do this? We're not Jesus. How can you and I have an attitudinal change? We're not God. Now can you and I love somebody we don't like? How can it happen? Can it happen? Jesus says that if we're to live his kind of life, if we're to have his kind of reaction to hostility, we've got to do what he does.

We're to love God. Now when Jesus is talking about God he is not talking about a formula. He is not talking about primal energy. He is not talking about a parallelogram. He is not talking about $E=MC^2$, he's talking about a person. You cannot love a thing. You can cherish a thing, but you love a person. You love a spirit, a mind, an attitude, a personification.

And God is spirit. He is not a thing—not just Mr. Power. He is not just the first cause. He is a person. If you and I are going to have an attitudinal change, if our spirits are ever going to be altered, if we're ever going to begin to love like God loved, we have to recognize that God is person, God is Spirit. And we are to love him. Not it, not the thing, not primal energy, not a formula, not an equation, but a person— Jesus Christ, personified God.

"He that hath seen me," said Jesus, "hath seen God." And Jesus is not like God—God is like Jesus. Jesus is not just God's afterthought, God's final expression with a better to come later. He is all the characteristics and qualities of God himself. Jesus is God.

If you and I are going to have an attitudinal change, it will begin when we see that God is in Christ reconciling us, changing our hearts, changing our attitudes. And Jesus said that we are to love God like he loved God. We are to love him with our whole personality, with all of our energies, with the totality of our personality. All of man's being, his moral nature, his emotion, his intellect, his psychic energy, his physical energy, must go into his love for God.

When we give God only a fraction of ourselves, God becomes a fraction of what he might be to us. If you only give God your mind, then your heart, your emotion, your physical energy stays out from under the controlling sway of Jesus Christ. If you give Jesus only your emotions, and you keep your mind, your spirit, your physical energies for yourself, then all of these areas of your life stay outside the area of God's grace.

One reason a lot of us are leading such crippled spiritual lives is because we think that all we've got to do to get to God is to give him our hearts, our souls. But we leave our minds, our physical energies, our intellect, our moral nature, everything but this emotional part of our being outside of the controlling grace of Jesus Christ.

When you enter a Moslem mosque, you leave your shoes outside the door. You don't wear your shoes inside. A lot of Christians leave their minds outside, and they think that all that God is interested in is that little part of them that's called emotion or spirit. If you and I are to have an attitudinal change, if we are to begin to love that which today we don't like, our minds have got to be changed, our attitudes have got to be changed. The totality of our personality must be submerged, baptized, in the spirit of God, or else God will be only a fraction of a power. If you do not give your mind, love becomes sentimental. If you do not give your heart, love becomes analytical. If you do not give your strength, love becomes theoretical.

Mind, heart, physical energy, the totality of your personality must be committed to Jesus Christ if you're to have an attitudinal change. God loved his unlovable neighbors. You—me—us. And his love for his unlovable neighbors expressed itself in a tangible manner. He gave his Son.

Now how does our love express itself? Do you love your neighbor? To love God without love for your neighbor is to disobey the scripture. The Bible says, "What God hath joined together let no man put asunder." Let no man divide. Let no man divorce. And God has put together love for him and love for your neighbor. He said if you don't love your neighbor, you don't love God. These are indivisible, inseparable. God has joined them together, and let no man divide them.

Without this total expression, love becomes a burden. It disengages the cross, turns it into a burden. The vertical beam still reaches up to God. Man's relationship to God. Man's conversation with God. Man's love for God. But there's a horizontal beam to the cross. Man's relationship to man, man's love for his fellowman. No more barriers, no more fences, no more walls. If you disengage this, you don't have a cross. It is impossible to have love for God without love for your fellowman, and it is futile to have love for your fellowman without love for God. The horizontal beam of the cross cannot be supported apart from the vertical relationship to God. But they must be engaged, and when they are engaged that cross becomes not a burden, but a power.

The cross is the kind of burden that an engine is to an automobile. It gives it power and strength. It's the kind of burden that sails are to a ship. It catches the power of the universe and translates it into direction. You can take that engine in your automobile, disassemble it, and try to carry it around by pushing the automobile. That's a burden.

And that's what's happening to a lot of our love. Our love for God has become disengaged from our love for the world, and we're just pushing our spiritual life around all of the time. We do not have the dynamic of the cross, we have the burden of a pole to carry, to drag. There must be engagement with God and with our fellowman if love is to be a dynamic. To love God alone bottles up, suppresses, represses that which is meant to be expressed, and love unexpressed will turn sour and die.

Look at a map of the Holy Land. There are two primary bodies of water. One is called the Sea of Galilee. It's not very large. You can stand on its banks and see all the way around it. It's a small body of water, but it's filled with history. Jesus walked its shores, tread upon its waters, called his disciples from its banks, centered his ministry in the area of the Sea of Galilee. It takes the cool melted snows of Mount Herman at its Northern shore, and in its Southern outlet, it drops those waters into the Jordan Valley.

But there's another body of water there. Further South,

much bigger. If size impresses you, you'd be very impressed. It takes the cool fresh waters of the Jordan in at its Northern shores and it holds them. It clutches every drop of fresh water that it can get and it hoards it. And what's it called? Any child in Sunday School can tell you what it's called. Dead Sea. Dead. Why is it dead? Because it doesn't give. It receives and receives and receives, but it never gives. And there's no life in it, and there's no life around it. So far as we know Jesus never visited it. He performed no miracles either on it or near it, he called no disciples from its shores. It's dead.

And that's the reason some of our lives are so lifeless, so devoid of vitality and power. We're always receiving, receiving, receiving. And if you do not express that love you have for God in a manner to your fellowman, if you do not translate this vertical emotion into horizontal service, you're dead.

No power, no vitality, no energy, no life because love to be love must express itself. Try to love your neighbor without love for God, and it becomes terribly frustrating because it's so terribly futile. The reason it is futile is because it has no eternal dimensions to it, no vertical relationships suspending it, giving it meaning, interpreting it, stabilizing it, and reaching above it. So if you try to love your fellowman without a corresponding love for God, it too becomes futile and phony and will degenerate into nothing more than meaningless manipulation of personalities.

You've heard the story about the Boy Scout who came back after having volunteered to do a good deed for the day. He came back bloody and bleeding. Someone asked him what was wrong, and he said, "Well, I helped a blind man across the street." They said, "Well, did a car run over you son?" He said, "No, he didn't want to go."

And if you try to love your fellowman and serve your fellowman without this eternal dimension, without the love of God in your heart prompting you and motivating you, you'll come back bloody and beaten all the time. It cannot be disengaged. What God has joined together let no man, let no church, put asunder. Love for God, love for your fellowman. They are two sides to the same coin, they're the two beams of the cross, they are inseparable and indivisible. How can this happen?

You've got to love yourself enough to let God into your life. Have you noticed that Jesus bases the whole thing upon love for yourself? He's not talking about egotism but about the need for some people to recognize what they are and who they are. And you feel unworthy? Listen. God considers you worthy. And Jesus Christ is inviting you to have at least the same opinion of yourself that God has of you.

He said, "You are to love your neighbor as you are to love yourself." You need to love yourself enough to let God come into your life. You need to quit exclaiming about your unworthiness because the cross shattered that. God said: "You are worth the death of my Son. Quit moping around here and being a paranoid masochist. I love you. Strong and powerful and virile love. I love you with all of my mind, with all of my heart, with all of my soul, with all of my strength, with all of my son, Jesus Christ, I love you."

Now let him into your life. Think enough of yourself to let God into your life. Have enough self evaluation to let Jesus Christ, the light and life of God come in because he believes you're worth it. You're worth Calvary. And if you had been the only sinner that ever lived, you would still have been worth it. Jesus Christ would have died for you. If you had been the only man or woman that had ever made a mistake, who ever told a lie, who ever coveted, who ever lusted, who ever used vile language, Jesus Christ would have died for you.

He loves you as though there is only one to love. He doesn't love all of us, he loves each of us. Separately, apart from everybody else in the world, he loves you, and he wants into your life. Do you think enough of yourself to let the God of the ages come in and live within your heart?

Jonas Salk, the discoverer of polio vaccine, said that people wouldn't take the vaccine, and he spoke to the Royal Congress of Health Society in England, "Polio vaccine has exposed one of the most important problems of the day. The responsibility that people do or do not take for their own welfare." If people don't act responsibly about polio, by the same token there are many people who don't do this about God.

You've got to have God in you to be Godlike. And I'm not talking about an inoculation, I'm talking about an incorporation. Christ in you. The hope of glory. And this becomes not imitation, but inspiration in-spirit-ation. God in you. You don't have to go around trying to imitate Christ. You can't do it. His stride's too long, and his steps are too big. You can't keep step with God. He doesn't ask you to. He says, "Let me get in you and your steps will become my steps." Not imitation. In-spirit-ation. Inspiration. Not duplication but dynamic. Something inside of you motivating you, giving you strength. Then the desire to follow Jesus Christ comes as the result of the spirit's compulsion rather than the demand of the law.

Jesus Christ is not a new Moses giving us a new law and becoming for us a new leader. That's not what it is at all. He is the Son of Man. He said, "And as the Son of Man, Son of God, I am going to come give you not a new law but a new spirit, not a new ideal but a new inspiration. A new person to live in you and to walk with you and to change your attitudes, to change your direction."

Can you imagine what kind of golfer you'd be if Arnold Palmer could live inside of you? I don't mean getting his books and reading them and going to a tournament and watching him and trying to duplicate his swing. You'd have his ability to read the green. You'd have his inner motivation for competition. You'd have available to you all of the accumulated experience that has been his across the twenty years of competitive golf. Just think what kind of golfer you'd be if Arnold Palmer could come live in you. Man, you'd walk on that first tee. You wouldn't have any friends when you got to eighteen, but boy, you'd have a lot of fun!

That can't happen. You know that can't happen. Suppose the spirit of Michelangelo could live in you. I don't mean you'd sit there and try to copy one of his paintings or some of his sculpture. I'm not talking about imitation. What if Michelangelo himself with all of his insight, his capacity, his feeling, his sensitivity, his eye for beauty could get inside of you? Great day. Think of the art you could produce. But that can't happen.

What if the spirit of Beethoven could live in you? Not just imitation. Not just listening to music and trying to duplicate it. He could live in you with his ear and his love of beauty. Think of the music you could produce. Well, that can't happen either.

Suppose a man who lived two thousand years ago who changed the world by the style of his life who loved his enemies, did good to them that hated him, lifted up the fallen, and liberated the oppressed came to live in you. That *can* happen. Arnold Palmer cannot, Michelangelo cannot, Beethoven cannot, but Jesus Christ can live in you.

You can have available all the eternal resources of God— all power in heaven and in earth. You can begin to see with different eyes and hear with different ears and walk with different feet and care because you're changed. Jesus Christ in you. Your attitudes change, your spirit changes, and that *can* happen.

9. Get Involved

What would you think of a person who refused, consciously and intentionally, to help an individual who was in danger of imminent death? What would you think? Jesus once said that if we pass by a suffering, needy, human being, whoever he might be, and whatever his need might be, if we pass him by, we cannot expect to possess eternal life. It is just that simple.

A certain teacher of the law came and tried to trap him. "Teacher," he asked, "what must I do to receive eternal life?" Jesus answered him, "What do the Scriptures say? How do you interpret them?" The man answered, "You must love the Lord your God with all your heart and with all your soul and with all your strength and with all your mind, and you must love your neighbor as yourself." "Your answer is correct," replied Jesus. "Do this and you will live." But the teacher of the law wanted to put himself in the right so he asked Jesus, "Who is my neighbor?"

Jesus answered, "A certain man was going down from Jerusalem to Jericho when robbers attacked him, stripped him, and beat him up, leaving him half dead. It so happens that a priest was going down that road, and when he saw the man he walked on by on the other side. In the same way a Levite also came by, went over and looked at him, and then walked on by on the other side. But a certain Samaritan who was traveling that way came upon him and when he saw him his heart was filled with pity. He went over to him, poured oil and wine on his wounds and bandaged them. Then he put the man on his own animal and took him to an inn where he took care of him. The next day he took out two silver coins and gave them to the innkeeper. "Take care of him," he told the innkeeper, "and when I come back this way I will pay you back whatever you spend on him."

And Jesus concluded, "Which one of these three seems to you to have been a neighbor to the man attacked by the robbers?" The teacher of the law answered, "The one who was kind to him." Jesus replied, "You go then and do the same."

To know that men die every day of hunger, that men and women and children live in hovels, ghettos, slums, some without any house at all, that some, in fact, many are unemployed, or receive next to nothing for a salary, that some men are forced to work under conditions that are little better than slavery, that men are illiterate, sick, forgotten. To know all of this and to do nothing about it amounts to condemning ourselves to eternal death, if what Jesus said is true. And what Jesus said is true. To know all of this and to do nothing about it is to damn our own souls.

Now in this life there's a lot of talk about loving God. We talk a great deal about it. But in this life there are not a lot of ways of loving God, only one. And that is to give ourselves to others, to love like God loved, to love what God loved, to love as God loved, to give ourselves to fellow human beings whoever they might be, and whatever their needs might be. Now there are a variety of ways of doing this to be sure, and this is the ministry that all of us have—to serve others in the name of Christ.

Now if you and I seek to develop our interior life to the exclusion of our exterior lives we are laboring under a very serious misapprehension. We cannot hope to be one with Jesus Christ in the silence of the Spirit if we leave the same Jesus Christ outside our relationships with a needy humanity.

If God has placed us in the world, if he intends us to be here and he intends us to stay here, he clearly intends that we say while we are here, "I have a responsibility, I have an obligation, I have a ministry to fulfil which would not be fulfilled were I absent."

We are not here to say to ourselves, "I have a vocation in life and that is just to help people spiritually." All about us, at home, at work, at school, in our neighborhood, there are people who are in need, who are waiting for us. You and I cannot evade the necessity of manifesting our love to them in specific, concrete, objective, individual, personal fashion.

Now it is certainly true that God does lead some individuals to more contemplation in their lives than he apparently does others. And I am convinced that contemplation and reflection play a very important, very necessary role in our lives. It grants a certain degree of peace of mind. It can impart knowledge which is a very good thing.

But, nevertheless, God never excuses anyone from a love which does not find expression, outward expression in the practical, concrete, specific, everyday deeds of personal helpfulness and service. Beware the subtle and fatal temptation to seek perfection, spiritual perfection, by fleeing from the world of other men and closing your eyes and your ears to the needs and cries of the world around us.

Very clearly, unmistakably, the Bible teaches that what you do in a specific way to help suffering humanity is evidence of the sincerity, the genuineness, and the authenticity of your love for God. For example, if you see a fight begin between two people, you ought to try to break it up and more than that, you ought to try to get those involved to come to some kind of understanding between one another. You ought to be a mediator between people.

When an epidemic breaks out, we don't just look after the sick. Certainly we do that. It's extremely important to do that. But we also try to get at the cause of the illness, the cause of the epidemic, the reason for the outbreak of the sickness. The sufferings of this world are the result of an almost infinite number of causes. And so you and I should be concerned not only about helping our sick and suffering brothers, we should certainly be concerned about them, but we should also try to get at some of the root causes of these sufferings.

Therefore, our efforts must involve the whole human life, the whole of contemporary society, and not just simply the individuals who live in that society, in that culture. The individual is of paramount importance. I'm not minimizing that, I'm not demeaning that. He is the area of our primary concern.

But also the institutions which comprise our society and our culture must be transformed as well. What are institutions? They are nothing but individuals who unite themselves together for a specific purpose. They have no entity apart from the individuals who constitute the membership, whether it is for government, for business, for education, or for worship. The institution is nothing but the collective spirit, the collective mentality, and the collective influence of its individuals.

We can give expression of our love for people by committing ourselves to them individually. It is extremely important, it's basic, it's paramount, but in addition to this, our acts of service, of witness, of involvement must also be directed to the entire community, the entire human family, the entire culture. And this can best be accomplished by the transformation of institutions through the witness of the church. The fellowship, the institution of the compassionate is brought together in the name of and in the spirit of Jesus Christ our Lord, our Savior, our leader.

Now this is part of the work of the church. Working not only as individuals infiltrating society, but working as a congregation witnessing to all of the institutions that comprise the world in which we live. This is part of the corporate ministry, the corporate work of the church. And this is something the church can do that you and I cannot do alone, that no individual can do alone.

But together we can become part of an institution that witnesses to and stands in a sense, in judgement upon, the institutions of our culture. Example: Perhaps a friend of yours is not getting along too well financially, and you've been rather successful. And so you make a generous sacrifice to help him. You give him some money, or you help him get a job, or you go on the note for him until he is able to get on his feet and do it himself. Something happens, circumstances conspire against him, and because he's your friend, you understand those circumstances. You don't blame him for it like we have a tendency to do.

You understand his situation, and so you see that there are circumstances involved over which he has no control which have produced this crisis in his life. You don't blame him for being broke or being poor, you help him. You help him. You are in that act performing the very Christian, wonderful, worthwhile, marvelous deed of Christian service. That's great. No doubt about it at all. You ought to do it.

But what about the many others who are in the same position as your friend? What about the root causes of all the difficulties? What about them? What about the root causes of injustice in our world? What about the root causes of inequality, poverty, ignorance? What about those? What are you and I going to do about those? Can we do anything about those?

Am I only to individually teach one child who wants to learn, or am I supposed to be so involved in my world as a Christian that I can do something about the many millions of children that I could never teach personally? Can't I be part of an institution or organization that is concerned not only with ministering to the individual, person to person but that can somehow do something about the system itself? Can we get at some of the root causes of these difficulties, these sufferings?

I believe so, therefore, our efforts must involve the whole of human life, the whole of contemporary society, and not just simply the individuals who comprise that society, though the individual is of paramount importance. These individual acts of Christian service do help other individuals, and they help them in a wonderful way, in a Christian way. But they can also be very, very deceptive if we are not careful because such acts of individual kindness, as indispensable as they are, can lead us subtly and insidiously to neglect the tremendous work that awaits us.

This work awaits us in the larger context of the entire community, city, nation, and world. The purpose of this work must be influencing and establishing institutions which respect the dignity of all human individuals and meet the demands for justice and equality for every man everywhere. And this is the

work that the church can do more effectively together than individually. Let me try to illustrate this further. There are many
fine Christian people in the South, elsewhere, too, but I'm a
child of the South. I've heard this all of my life. Maybe you've
even said it or heard your parents say it, "Some of my best
friends are Negroes."

"My mother and father were very kind to this family or
that family, or to these specific Negro individuals." That's
good. That's very fine, very noble, very Christian. But at the
same time, many of these individuals, because they know a
certain person, or because they have been around a certain
family help an individual Negro or Negro family.

Yet they would and they do, at the same time ignore social
and economic conditions and educational limitations which
produce the kind of person who needed their help in the first
place. You see individual service, however Christian it might
be can never be a substitute for my own personal involvement
in the changing of the structures of our world that contribute
to the destruction of any man, anywhere.

Let's suppose for example that you've seen a robbery take
place. If you don't do anything to stop it or if you refuse to
identify the criminal even though you got a very good look at
him, you become the criminal's accomplice, and you deserve
the same treatment as he. Isn't that right?

Now! Through our life in this society, we are witness to
many, many acts in which love and justice and fair play have
no part at all, and we know it. Many acts bring suffering and
privation to a great many people. Now if you and I don't
speak up, if we do not individually and collectively say something, if we do not act as the body of Christ in the twentieth
century, if we do not identify those causes which contribute to
this kind of evil, if we do not do anything to change the social

structure which produces ignorance and inequality and injustice, then you and I become an accomplice. The guilt of those crimes rests upon us as well.

Neutrality is a vicious form of opposition. If we don't give monetarily to the church of Jesus Christ, if we do not give ourselves to the ministries, the work, the influence, and the outreach of the church, then we become an accomplice with those who would destroy the message of Christ if they could. Our neutrality becomes an insidious form of opposition.

Now, when confronted with human suffering you strive and work as hard as your circumstances will permit, not only to offer help, but also to lay the axe to the root of the problem. However, do not be led into the opposite error of working solely at the causes of injustice without offering help to those who are now its victims.

If everybody had enough to eat, if everybody had a roof over his head, if everybody had an education, a car, a refrigerator, if everybody had a decent job, if science and technology had given us mastery over our environment, if medicine had given us victory over all of the diseases that plague man, if the political and economic institutions of society were equally just to all men everywhere, would the earth be a paradise of unalloyed and uncomplicated happiness? No, it would not. Not if the heart of man remains unchanged. Not if the heart of man remains impenitent and unconverted.

We must strive in every way possible to make of present society a place where life can be lived at its fullest and freest and best. Certainly we must be concerned about that, but at the same time we must guard against falling into the illusion that social reform and social change by itself can guarantee a man's salvation. It cannot.

What, then, should we start with? Where should we begin? With man and his attitudes, or society and its institutions?

This is the question the church faces today, and I personally do not know why it is so hard for us to hear the answer. Here it is written on the pages of the New Testament. It is written as large as the life of Jesus Christ. Where does the church begin? Both places? Both places. Who cleansed the temple in Jerusalem? Who turned over the tables? Who upset public decorum? Jesus Christ did. Who died on the cross for man's sins? Jesus Christ did. I would to God that we could see that we're to begin both places. This is what the incarnation means. This is what God has been trying to say to us through Jesus Christ for 2000 years.

It's not a question or either/or. You begin both places. You cleanse the temples, and you take up the cross. Work collectively in the life of the culture, work individually in the lives of disciples. Both are needed. And we are his body, we are his workmanship created in Christ Jesus for good works in which God has already ordained that we should walk. And we ought to be doing exactly what Jesus did, and that's what the incarnation is trying to say to us. That's what the good news is all about.

Here is God's eternal spirit joining itself to human form, being born in a manger, growing up a carpenter, cleansing temples, saving individuals. That's what we're to do. This is what the church is supposed to be involved in during the twentieth century. He's our answer. Don't forget that in the end it is man who must be transformed. Man must be transformed.

The soul of all renewal is the renewal of the soul, but that's not all there is to it. Not all by any means. Therefore, every work that is done, whether individual or collective, every deed that is done, whether an act of individual kindness or the involvement of a Christian in the structures of society, everything that's done, look at it. Everything that is done, whether you eat or drink, whatsoever you do, do all for the glory of

God, in the name of Jesus Christ. You see, man is a unified whole. Greek philosophy has divided him into two or three parts. The Bible knows nothing of this kind of division, biblical theology knows nothing of this kind of division of body, soul, and spirit. The Bible sees man as a whole.

And so you and I looking at man with a biblical view recognize that it is essential that by using many kinds of methods we try to save the whole man. Not just his body today and his soul tomorrow, but the whole man.

It becomes our responsibility, our opportunity, and our vocation to point men to the Lamb of God which taketh away the sin of the world. That's what churches are supposed to be and that's what they're supposed to do. To reach the whole man with the redeeming, healing message of Jesus Christ. The message of reconciliation. Here it is, "For God was in Christ," doing what? "Reconciling the world unto himself."

10. The Place of the Church

Christianity was anything but a respectable creed in its beginning. Its founder moved among the outcasts of society, the prostitutes, racial minorities, political traitors, misfits, vagrants, and thieves. He was at home among the hungry, the naked, and the imprisoned. He himself was considered a religious heretic, a traitor to his nation, an enemy to the status quo. He was a man who broke the Sabbath, a dangerous radical, a disturber, a malcontent who fought the establishment. His constant companions were hardly the sort of people one finds today in our churches on Sunday morning. And when he stood trial, there was an element of truth in the accusation under which he was indicted, "He stirred up the people." And he did.

Three times in the series of conflicts recorded in Mark 2, we read questions beginning with the word, why. The question was addressed either to Jesus or to the followers of Jesus by the Pharisees, the good people of the day, the church going folks of the day. They asked this question because Jesus was getting out of hand. They were saying in so many words, "Why can't you keep your teacher in place?" "Why can't you keep your teacher within decent limits? Why can't you make him more respectable like us?"

One could scarcely call him success motivated, not only by present standards but by the standards of his own day as well. He was anything but a roaring success, in fact, he was more of a failure. He went to his degrading death broken and beaten, cast out by respectable society, spat upon and cursed by the righteous.

And it appeared when he died that he had accomplished next to nothing. In fact it would have been very difficult to prepare a suitable caption to publish beneath his photograph in any church publication had any such publication existed at that time. And because he was the way he was, he was the great upsetter. And because he is the way he was, unchanging, eternal, the same yesterday, today, and forever, he is still the great upsetter, the great disquieter, the great disturber.

We don't like to see him like this because we prefer to seal him off in the antiseptic corner of our Sunday morning activities, but he refuses to stay there. He refuses to be confined and comes breaking out. When he does, our hearts like the hearts of those good folks long ago, often merely stand in wonder and stammer, "Why, why, why, why?"

The religious establishment of Jesus' day had a fellowship, but they had a fellowship really that was too small to hold the sinner. It made its own definition of who was right. It made its own definition of who was in. They just couldn't find room in their church for people who had obvious problems.

If you could disguise your problems well enough and could somehow cover up with a religious veneer, if you could learn a few religious words, a few religious cliches, a little church jargon, you could camouflage the depravity of your own heart. If you could do that successfully enough, then you could get in. But if you were honest enough and recognized that you had some flaws in your character and some skeletons in your closet, then you'd be blackballed; you couldn't make it, you wouldn't qualify.

You can see why folks like this would be upset when Jesus came along. There was nothing they could do but say, "Why, why, why, look what he's doing. Here's a man who's saying that his fellowship just will not be limited, and we cannot tolerate a man like that."

And he's still saying that. We don't believe it very well, and we practice it even less, but Jesus is still saying that. He settled the limits of responsibility long before he ever went to Calvary. The word, world, was forever on his lips. World, not my people, my kind, my folks, *world*. "You are the light of the world." "Go ye therefore into all the world, all the kingdoms of the world. I am the light of the world. Light has come into the world."

And the message he came to deliver was a message for all men regardless. He said, "if *any* will come after me," if *any*. Some say that the words "if any" are the greatest words in the gospel because they are the words that make the gospel. If any. And the church that stops short of the boundaries of Jesus is a church that has not followed its Lord.

In this connection, I'm thinking of a church that worked out a method of limiting the attendance of lower classes in their congregation by an expedient gimmick. They established a special department that meets at the same time everybody else meets, but it meets across the street in a basement. It is away from the large sanctuary where the more respectable members of society have gathered to worship their tribal deity. Thus the unwashed are effectively constrained from wandering into the stained glass ghetto which the best people had built for themselves and for themselves alone.

And honesty makes me question whether we may be doing the same thing. What is our motivation for missions? What is it? Around the world, what is our motivation for missions? Is it the outstretched hand of compassion or is it the stiff arm of exclusivism? Which is it? Our Lord is not only interested in what we do, he's interested in why we do it, too. And we can do the right thing in the wrong way, and it can turn us into demons rather than saints.

What would Jesus reply to this question? We read in Mark 2:17, "Those who are well have no need of a physician, but those who are sick. I came not to call the righteous but sinners." Now this may have been sarcasm. On occasion Jesus employed sarcasm and did so with devastating force.

It's as though Jesus is saying, "All right, so you are the goodies. You're the righteous, very good, but I came to call sinners. I'm not going to argue with you. You've closed your mind and an argument won't open a closed mind. It'll just cement it. If you're so blind to yourself that you refuse to see, there is no man so blind as one who refuses to see. We'll just let it go at that. I came to call those who are crying out for help; the sick, the sinner, the outcast, the disinherited, the ignored. I came for them." And it is strange, that the followers of Jesus bound together in the church that bear his name could ever forget this exciting word, this simple purpose, that he came to "seek and save that which was lost."

What would we think of the crew of a life-saving station who gave all of their attention to the station itself? They made the quarters attractive, planted gardens, designed uniforms, provided music, and thus pleasantly occupied themselves. They shut out the roar of the pounding waves that were driving men to destruction on the rocks all about them. What would we think of a live-saving station like that?

Why, we'd say, "It's incredible, it's unbelievable." Yet it's not too incredible, nor is it too far removed from a disquieting description of the modern church. A modern church that is so intent on its own life, its housing, its decoration, its material well being, that the plight of those outside in need of salvation, in need of rescue, are breaking on the rocks all about. Why, the church is not a company of vacationers seated on the front porch of a summer hotel. It's a life-saving crew. It's supposed to be.

How many churches, just at the moment when the world needs them the most, just when the problems about them are growing great, pack up and follow the righteous out to some pleasant location in a residential neighborhood where peace, perfect peace, reigns. And in some such fashion they get away from the disturbing cries of broken hearts and burdens of sin and need down where people really live and where life's decisions are really made, down where we, unfortunately seldom get. And trying to save our life we can lose our souls, and what will it profit us?

The Pharisees came again. Jesus did something they didn't like, and they came again, stammering, "You're getting out of hand, you're getting out of hand. Don't you know that you're not supposed to act like that? You're saying by your actions and by your works that the message you preach is good news of love for everybody. Why do you do this? Don't you know better? Why don't you fast? Why don't you observe all the rules we've made, all of the regulations we've set up, why don't you do this?"

It's easy to understand the attitude of these Pharisees, especially for some of us because we're so much like them. Men whose feet were firmly cemented in the present and whose minds were unalterably committed to the past, men who had a stiff religious legalism that was too brittle to hold any new truths, eyes too blind to see new light. It's easy to understand them because in varying degrees all of us in the religious establishment are somewhat like them.

When we can have the courage to see ourselves, we will see this about us. We can see, for example, how the Protestant church, how the Baptist church, still clings to its somber, puritan past. It still subconsciously believes that everything gay or colorful or enjoyable is somehow sinful. If it's fun, it's wrong. Fast, gay music is wrong. Rhythm is especially sinful because it somehow connotes dancing. Bright colors are sinful. Jokes are sinful because they are frivolous and, of course, all frivolity is sin. Adornment of all kinds is sinful.

I recognize that the church no longer consciously believes all of these specifics. But if you don't already know it and recognize it, the impression that the church gives to the world is that we *do* believe such things. And out of the dark recesses of our joyless past these ingrained notions emerge like small, elusive demons to haunt us and these demons need to be exorcized.

Has the church forgotten that Christianity, in its original version, is meant to be a joyful religion with its inherent promise of unconditional forgiveness and unconditional love? We're involved in a marriage feast, not in a funeral. Have we forgotten that? If we have not, why does the church make such a virtue of black?

Jesus answers the questions of these Pharisees by saying, "You don't put new wine in the old wineskins. If you do the wine will burst the skins and the skins and the wine will be lost." And the meaning of what Jesus said is very clear. The good news of the kingdom of God cannot be captured in old forms, in old rules, in old negativism, it just cannot be held there, it will come bursting out into life.

And then the third question the Pharisees asked, the third why, was "Why do you violate the sabbath? Do you realize that you and your disciples were going to the corn fields, having a good time, eating the grain, and forgetting all about the rules? God gave the rules, and you forgot them. You're doing something that's against the law—our law."

Now it's understandable why these Pharisees would ask such a question because these were sincere men, good men in many ways.

They had a view of goodness that was too limited to offer loving service anytime, anywhere, to anybody. They believed in being good, but at the right time, the right place, to the right folks. And they had a limited concept of service, and they tried to force Jesus into this. Therefore, they came into conflict with Jesus.

We also can come into conflict with him. Because he has a service that just will not be regulated. He has a compassion that just would not wait for the proper day and the proper time, the proper place and the proper person. He ministered on any day at any time to anybody in any condition. And they couldn't countenance that. They simply did not have a large enough concept of service to agree with Jesus' evaluation. Therefore, they asked him the question—why?

Jesus provides a test for all institutions including those of the Christian religion itself. A test of all institutions: the schools, the hospitals, the church, the Sunday School, the Training Union, any institution, any form. He provides a test for it, and it is this, "Does it serve men?"

If it does not, then it is a failure, and it is a miserable failure. It may be big, it may be prosperous, it may be effective in its organization, but if it doesn't serve man, it's not Christian! No institution is sacred in itself. People are sacred, *people*. And any authority and any sanctity that an institution deserves comes from its service to human needs.

How many times in outlook and in action have men been forgotten? How often has the church, dominated by the illusion that it is sacred in itself been occupied with power and with pageantry and lost sight of the fact that the only true authority lies in its service to the needs of man. "Inasmuch as ye have done it unto one of the least of these, my brethren."

Jesus' answer to his accusers' question of "why, why, why," was this: "I have a fellowship that just will not be limited. I have a gospel that will not be restricted. I have a service that will not wait. And those who follow me must practice this kind of gospel. Anything less than this is not gospel, not the gospel of Jesus Christ. And if anyone preach any other gospel than this, let him be anathema, but if a man will believe this good news and practice this good news, he will be saved."

For Jesus is saying that there are no sins which eliminate us, no work that disqualifies, no problem that ostracizes, none at all. And the Lord has said a thousand times: "I don't care what you are, I don't care what you have been, I don't care what you have done, I don't care what you are doing. You're not going to make me blush. Come on. Come on in and I will take your burdens, take your sins, take your failure, that's my business."

No limitation to it. It's for everybody and anybody, that's why it's good news. There aren't laws to restrict us. Nowhere in the kingdom of God can we find any "No Trespassing" signs, no law to eliminate us. This gospel comes bursting out of these laws as a spring of life within us, and it obliterates all the past, it redeems all the future, it satisfies all the present.

Finally Christ says, "If you come to me everything in the divine economy is at your disposal, and all of your needs will be met, all of the deepest desires of your heart will be satisfied. Nothing, not your sins, not society's laws will keep me from meeting the needs of your heart and the needs of your life, if you'll just come. We'll turn on all the lights, we'll start the music, we'll begin the party, we'll clean you up, we'll put a new coat on your back, new shoes on your feet, a ring on your finger, we'll kill the fatted calf, and we'll live. I came to give you this kind of life."

"I can give it to you more abundantly than you've been living off the scraps down there in the prodigal's pen. Come on home for the first course of divine dinner's being served. Come on and live. Know the joy of redemption and acceptance and forgiveness and reinstatement into the life of the family of God. Come on home."

It is to follow this kind of Christ that we invite you now.

11. "For the Living of These Days"

I suppose every pastor or speaker has had the experience of bringing a message and after the message is over having someone say, "You know, in your message you said so and so." I don't contradict them on the spot because God used some word or some impression or some thought to say that word to their heart and that's what they heard and that's what they needed to hear. But I didn't say exactly what they said I said. That's one genius among many others of the Spirit of God. To take this truth and fit it to each heart and to each life as we have need.

It was he who gave gifts to men, Paul writes in Ephesians 4. He appointed some to be apostles, others to be prophets, others to be evangelists, others to be pastors and teachers. He did this to prepare all God's people for the work of Christian service. He did this not to prepare apostles and evangelists and prophets and pastors and teachers for Christian service.

These people, these ministries, these individuals, these insights are gifts—gifts of the Spirit of God to the church, to you, to the people of God. He did this to prepare all of God's people for the work of Christian service—to build up the body of Christ—you.

Paul said, "And so we shall all come together to that one-ness in our faith and in our knowledge of the Son of God. We shall become mature men—reaching to the very height of Christ's full stature. Then we shall no longer be children, carried by the waves and blown about by every shifting wind of the teaching of deceitful men who lead others to error by the tricks they invent. Instead, by speaking the truth in a spirit of love, we must grow up in every way to Christ, who is the head. Under his control, all the parts of the body fit together, and the whole body is held together by every joint with which it is provided. So when each separate part works as it should, the whole body grows and builds itself through love."

About six years ago, I was coming back from a retreat in the hill country of Texas. I was with a very close friend of mine, a deacon in our church, a fine Christian businessman. I'd known him nearly all of my life. His father and my father were college friends, and we have a very good, honest personal relationship. I said to him, "Man, wasn't that a terrific retreat?" There I was, bulging with notes and sermon ideas, illustrations, and with the good food that we had eaten. It was a great retreat.

He was not being cynical—he's not a cynic, he was not bitter—he just was being honest. He and I are such friends that we can afford the luxury of honesty with each other. He said, "Yeah, Buckner, it was good, but I want to tell you something. I've had all the inspiration I can stand. I've taken my last note. I've remembered my last point. I've been importing and I am satiated. I have been receiving, I have been taking in, I have been getting ideas, I have been getting inspiration, I'm through. Buckner, unless you and/or the church can give me a handle whereby I can start translating some of these ideas, this concern, and this inspiration into some practical deeds of Christian ministry, I've had it."

That shook me up. Because I knew down deep inside that I'd been thinking that for a long, long time. And he said it. And so I asked God to let some of the ideas and the theology and the impressions that were resident within my heart and present within the word of God, surface. And I began to see that the church, God's people, God's body, that every member of the church, every Christian is a minister of Christ. And a part of my role as pastor, is to minister to you, who are the ministers. I have many ministries in the world, but one of my primary ministries is as I minister to the minister. For every Christian is a minister.

You have a ministry as surely as Billy Graham or any missionary on the foreign field. You are as called of God to be a witness to Christ and a minister of Christ as anyone who stands in the pulpit. He gave some prophets and apostles and evangelists and pastors and teachers to prepare everybody for the work of Christian service. You are a minister.

And a pastor's role to the church is like that of a prompter to a play. The prompter to the play isn't out there in the middle of the stage acting out all of the parts, saying all of the lines, and going through all of the motions. The prompter stands over there behind the curtain. And there are a multitude of people in the cast, and they are communicating the idea, each one saying his own words. If he stumbles, if he hesitates, if he forgets, if he needs encouragement, the prompter's there. Feeding him the lines, inspiring, and encouraging him. The pastor is to the church like a prompter to a play or a coach to a football team. There are no spectators in the cause of Christ. There are no grandstand spectators in the game of life. Everybody's a participant. Some people have been in training longer than others, some people are more adroit at one form of service than another, but everybody's on the team. Nobody's sitting up in the grandstand except those who have already graduated to glory. Everybody else is a part of a team.

There are no passengers on board this ship. Everybody is a member of the crew. Everybody's to shoulder his responsibility. Everybody's to get hold of his work and perform it for Jesus Christ. You are a minister.

As ministers therefore, what are we to do? Jesus said we are servants. The greatest among you, he said, shall be a servant. Once you get to be a servant you can no longer choose who you are going to serve. A servant doesn't have the prerogative of picking who he will serve and who he will not serve. A servant doesn't decide where he will serve or when he will serve or what he will serve—he serves. It's not always attractive, it's not always appealing, it may not be pleasant due to your background or even to some of your prejudices, but you are not your own.

You no longer have the prerogative of choosing who you'll serve—not if you belong to Jesus Christ. You're not your own. You have been bought. You are a slave, and you serve. Wherever he says serve, whomever he says serve, whatever he says serve, whenever he says serve, you serve. This can sometimes be very threatening. It can be even frightening. It can create despair. It can make some of us begin to walk by faith when most of our lives we've been walking by sight. It can be terrifying.

But it is electrifying—with the Spirit of God. Buildings like our bodies are dedicated to God. I beseech you therefore brethren by the mercies of God that you present your body, dedicate your body a living sacrifice, your individual body, the collective body of the church, the buildings in which the church meets—dedicated to God. Whenever you dedicate something to God, you lose control over it. If you maintain control, you haven't given it to God. If you try to maintain control over the work of the body of Christ in the world, you haven't given it to God.

We as Christians then begin to see something together, as we learn, work, pray, and serve where God would have us. We begin to see that the church is not a building. It's not carpet, it's not wood, it's not stone, it's you. You're the body. You are the church. You are the fellowship, you are the servants, you are the bride, you are the people of God. You are the household of faith. You are the family of God. You're it.

It's hard to change your language when you see that you have been speaking some heresy really. My children say, "Daddy where are you going?" I say I'm going to the church. I'm not *going* to the church! I *am* the church.

Wherever I am and wherever you are the church is. Certainly sometimes the church comes together collectively. We are the fellowship met to study and to pray, to have fellowship, to break bread together, to worship, to praise God, but we are no less the church on Monday morning than we are on Sunday morning. We are just the church scattered in the world. Just the church at work, just the church ministering. And as we see this, we realize the criteria of Christian dedication should no longer be those who are there every time the doors are open. In fact I've said to church members, "If you're there every time the doors are open, you are there too much."

We begin to see that the real criteria of Christian service is not those who are there every time the doors are open, but those who are there every time the doors are closed.

Where is the real battle for the souls of men being fought?

At the corner of what's-its-name and what's-its-name on Sunday morning? That's just a refueling spot. Where's the real battle for the souls of men being fought? In the world where you are—where you're a minister. In that office building, in that home, in that classroom, in the service, or wherever you are, that's where the water hits the wheel, that's where Christ sent you. That's the world he commissioned you to go into. Jesus Christ sent us into all of our world to minister there for Jesus Christ. And we come back together again to strengthen, encourage, and learn from one another and say "Stay in there man, you're doing a great job down there at the life insurance company or there in the schoolroom, or wherever it is." And we come to see that the church is something of a service station.

Why do you go to a service station? I pull into the service station pretty regularly. I stop there and they come out and fill the car with gasoline, check the oil and the tires, wipe off the windshield and occasionally they'll sweep out the inside if they're not too busy. After I've gotten the automobile filled with gas and spoken to my friends where I trade, and visited there a little while, I get back in the car. Then what do I do? Do I sit there all day long? Do I sit there and say "Oh, I just love to sit here in this service station?" No, I've been serviced, now I must get out of there and burn up that fuel.

What's a church? A place we come to? Yes, in a sense, but only so we can get somewhere else. And the real proof of what happens on Sunday morning is the quality of life lived on Monday morning out there in the world. You come together on Sunday to be filled with the power of God and have the windshield of your vision cleansed, the oil of the spirit checked, and be sure that the wind of the spirit fills those tires, so that you can do what? Get out of there and burn up that fuel on the expressways of life accomplishing something for Jesus

Christ. Begin to see this. Begin to see it together, and church will become exciting! Worship, Sunday School, prayer meeting, choir rehearsal, and everything that we do is something that equips, instructs, and encourages us. There the fields are white unto harvest, and we know that while we are out there either individually or collectively, that behind us is a great company of men and women who are praying for us, lifting us up before the Lord.

12. One Church at Work

In Chapter 2, I mentioned some of the activities of my church, Trinity Baptist in San Antonio. These were not related to magnify what we are doing. Nor do I mean that every other church should try to copy our program. I share with you out of my experience—out of the experience of the congregation where I serve as pastor—to let you know that real Christian service is possible where you live.

Many—even most—of the conditions where you live may be different from ours. Likely enough, there is not one other church anywhere that should try to do exactly what we are trying to do. Yet, wherever you are, whatever your circumstances, you have your own opportunities. Let me share further with you to illustrate some of the ways we have come to see the opportunities that were open around us. Since God has led us to see these things, I believe that he can and will lead you—if you are willing to open your eyes and your heart.

At Trinity Church, some people said, "Why don't we start a coffee house, why don't we take the gospel out there where there are servicemen? There are thousands of them in San Antonio on liberty there on North St. Mary's."

"Hey, that's a great idea."

"What will we call it?"

"Well let's don't call it anything that sounds so churchy that we won't be able to witness before we talk. 'My works testify of me'—isn't that what Jesus said?"

We were able to find a place right next door to the Green Gate Lounge, one of the biggest striptease joints in San Antonio. We decided to call it The Door. And one Sunday night I said, "How many people here would like to endeavor to minister for Christ in a way that's altogether different from anything we've done before? I'm not talking to Sunday School teachers. You have all you are doing and that's your ministry and that's your work for right now. How many others of you would like to do something for Christ in a unique ministry where all it takes is a willingness to meet people and to let yourself be questioned about what you believe? Not telling somebody but letting somebody else ask you. Stay after church."

Do you know how many people stayed? Forty. Most of them were people who were challenged by something different and something difficult.

The story of The Door in itself would make an exciting book. The miracles that took place in people's lives that gave coffee and cookies and cake. We had a big Thanksgiving Dinner there, a seated dinner for thirty-five people and went out and invited all the people that had to work on Thanksgiving Day. We had all kinds of people there—bellboys from the hotel, newsboys, a dope pusher off Houston Street, kids that worked in the bus station half a block away. Before we sat down to a dinner provided by the membership of the church, I said, "We are here because Jesus Christ cared about us and we care about you. We've come together to thank God for all of these blessings, and we invite you to eat." It was a fantastic experience.

Congregations today realize that they are to go into all of the world. The need is the call and the greater the need, the greater the responsibility for the Christian to be there, individually and collectively. People say, "Preacher, give us a handle." Well, people can find handles. And the church can minister imaginatively and creatively in the world.

Let me tell you some further details about some of the things I mentioned in Chapter 2.

A woman called me one afternoon, and said "I want you to go to a certain address, and I just want you to see what's happening there. I'm not going to tell you any more about it than that there's an alcoholic over there, a woman, who's been dry —that means she hasn't had a drink—for nearly a year. She's trying to take care of three other alcoholics who've just been released into her custody out of the county jail. Just go look at it."

Well, I went to look at it, and I've never seen anything like it. They had no lights, no electricity, no heat, no water. It was an old dilapidated mission. It had at one time been an abortion mill. It was bad, bad news. I went back and called three men in our church and I said, "Would you fellows just go look?"

I didn't hear any more about it for a day-and-a-half. One of the men called me and said, "Buckner, three of us went over there. We got together and paid the rent for two months and moved them over on Magnolia." That was the start of what has since become Alpha Home.

The whole process of rehabilitation is involved—mentally, spiritually, and physically. We have a group of men in the church who endeavor to get the women jobs after they've reached a certain place, a certain plateau in their process of recovery. I have baptized into the fellowship of Trinity Baptist Church women who have been won to Christ because of Alpha Home.

Alpha Home became a focal point, and God began to open up whole vistas of service, ideas. We have a benevolence house. We bought a house to do nothing but house the food and the clothing that our members bring to give to other people. There's not an affluent congregation today who couldn't fill a house with discarded clothes. We feed and clothe hundreds of people each year. Hundreds. There are twelve families that are able to live, able to live and go to school and function because of the work of the benevolence house.

We have three local missions. We have schoolteachers who have volunteered to go over every afternoon after school to conduct study hall at our missions. Eighty percent of the juvenile delinquents in San Antonio are school dropouts. They come from overcrowded conditions and from homes that do not understand the necessity of an education or anything about the need for homework. So we've bought reference books, we have air-conditioned rooms, well-lighted. Teachers and our older young people go there to tutor.

We had a bad flood in San Antonio a few years ago, and we gave a lot of food and clothing to people whose homes were destroyed. Why shouldn't the church be concerned about flood control as well as flood relief? I said to Trinity Baptist Church, "Why don't some of you men get on the San Antonio River Authority, and the City Council? Run for political office and get involved in some of these causes of human need in our community. As a Christian be involved."

In 1960, Jim Ruble, a layman from our church, went to Jamaica on a preaching mission. Since then one week out of the year we have had teams of laymen to go to Jamaica to spend a week preaching. There are eight churches in Jamaica where we work and minister and encourage. Our church buys all the Sunday School literature for these churches. They had no Sunday Schools. The two pastors didn't have cars so they could get to only one or two churches a Sunday. So we bought each of them an automobile so they could make all four of their churches, their whole circuit each Sunday. They have baptized hundreds of people. Laymen are now involved ministering in Jamaica because of the influence of a group of men, who at their own expense, their own time, spend the week on the island of Jamaica, sharing with these people what Jesus Christ has done for them.

The women of our church have led in a very exciting, meaningful way, and I thank God for them. They were the first to begin Mission Action Groups. They're working in the areas of juvenile rehabilitation, and in many areas beyond that. A group called Headliners is working with the aged, working with hospitals, and in other ways.

Jesus said, "You are the salt of the" . . . *church?* No. "You are the salt of the *earth.*" "You are the light of the" what? Light of the church? No. "You are the light of the *world.*" "Go into all of the *world.*" You see that's the way the salt has to be shaken out. The strength of the salt is not in the salt shaker. That's not the dynamic. The dynamic is when that salt shaker shakes everybody out on Sunday afternoon and Sunday night and Monday into the life of the community and they begin to season life. And purify life. And excite life, as the salt of the earth.

On December 15, 1968, our church accepted the responsibility of a Children's Home in Bexar County. Bexar County

Commissioner's Court had closed the Children's Home for dependent, neglected children. The only place for those children to go was then the State Reform School, which was bad.

It's staffed now by trained social workers, house parents. We provide all the food, all the clothing, education, recreation, worship, dental care—our dentists providing all the dental care, our doctors providing the medical care. Some have these children as foster children in their homes at least one weekend a month. What we said to the church was, "We don't want to just support financially another institution, that's not what we need. We need to get our own hands on the needs of the world." Isn't that what a servant does? A servant doesn't plan meals. He serves meals.

There's more unused space during the week in church Sunday School buildings than in any other place in America. Buildings lie dormant all week long. Why not a literacy program? Why not courses in hygiene? Now I know the defense mechanism that is employed when we begin talking about things like this: "Wait a minute! That's social gospel!" No sir, it's gospel. It spells itself out in human needs. Wherever there was need, there was Jesus Christ, and wherever we go, we go in his name and in his spirit. The first Christians went everywhere, sharing, preaching, testifying, witnessing—everywhere.

I'd be very untrue to you and untrue to myself if I said this was simple or easy or another gimmick. It's not that. But I believe it's the will of God that we go everywhere sharing. Broaden your concept of evangelism. Broaden your concept of Christian service. Let God liberate your imagination, free your spirit, and be a servant. Save your life, you'll lose it, but lose your life for Jesus' sake, and you'll find it.

13. What in the World
Are You Doing?

You and I live in an age of obliteration. We live among one of the greatest crises of human history. Not only war, but racism, famine, pestilence, revolution, and a legion of other calamities are also rampant over the whole world. All values are unsettled, all norms are broken. Humanity has become a distorted image of its own noble self. We're like a man getting drunk at his own funeral, we're like a sundial on a stormy day, we cannot tell the time.

For whatever consolation it might be, we're not the only century in human history that has felt such tension, such restlessness, such uncertainty. The first century, in many ways, was much like the twentieth century, and the disciples within the first century were much like the disciples of the twentieth century. Asking Jesus, "Is the time over, is this the fulfillment, are you going now to restore the kingdom to Israel, will we have no more crucifixions, will we have no more turmoil, are

upheavals to cease?" And Jesus' answer to those restless and
fearful followers in the first century is the same answer that he
gives to the restless, fearful, uncertain followers in the twentieth century. When the apostles met together with Jesus, they
asked him in Acts 1, following his resurrection, "Lord, will
you at this time give the kingdom back to Israel? Is this the
consummation of all things? Are we going to have peace?
And ease, and prosperity?"

Jesus said to them, "The times and occasions are set by the
Father's own authority. It is not for you to know what they
will be. But you will be filled with power when the Holy Spirit
comes on you, and you will be witnesses for me in Jerusalem
and in all Judea, and Samaria and to the ends of the earth."
Try to get this picture. These were disciples, all of whom had
forsaken him and fled, as the New Testament teaches us, on
the night of his arrest. They were ripped by fear, cowardice
overcame them, and they fled. And it is to this group of unpredictable men, men who had been terribly afraid, that Jesus
says, "You shall receive power. It's to come to you. And the
reason that you are able now to receive it is because you
recognize that in your own strength, you're insufficient. When
left to yourself you run, you hide. You have now recognized
your inability to cope with the situations that face you. Now
you're ready for my kind of power. Now you're ready to receive my kind of life. Now you're ready to live like I'm going
to empower you and enable you to live. You're ready for it."

He is saying that we find ourselves in the same emotional
and mental condition that these first disciples were in. "I am
going to give you a new kind of power." There's a great deal of
talk of power in our day, the power of the tyrant, the power of
the Caesar, armed strength, armed might. That's not what
he's talking about. "I am going to give you a new kind of
power for God hath not given us the spirit of fear, but of

power and of love, and of a sound mind." Isn't that a great verse? God hath not given us the spirit of fear, Timothy. We're being run out of town, hounded, resisted, persecuted, and we ultimately may be murdered, but God has not given us the spirit of fear.

Caesar is saying, "You are to obey my laws or you die. You are to say, 'Caesar is Lord,' or you go to prison." And Paul's saying, "I'll not say 'Caesar is Lord.' There is a higher power, there's a higher authority, and to it I will give my allegiance." God hath not given us the spirit of fear. We're not going to cower before all of the Caesars of the world. God has not given us the spirit of fear, but power, and love, and a sound mind. The power of love doesn't strut, it doesn't make a big display or show. It just gives and serves and helps. He ministers and lifts and heals and blesses and loves.

There are many things about Napoleon I do not admire. But he said some remarkable things, one of which is a statement about the love of Christ. "Caesar, Alexander, Charlemagne, and I have founded empires. Upon what did we rest the creation of our genius? Upon force. Force. Jesus Christ alone founded his empire upon love, and today, millions would die for him. I die before my time and my body will be given to the worms. Such is the fate of him who has been called 'the great Napoleon.' What an eternal abyss between my deep misery and the eternal kingdom of Christ, which is love proclaimed and adored throughout the whole world. Call you this dying? No, he is rather living."

You're wrong about many things, Napoleon, but right about Jesus. He is living to give loving power. "Ye shall receive that which is yours. It is your inheritance, it is your birthright as a child of God. Ye shall receive a new kind of power because you're going to be captured by a new spirit. Not the spirit of the world, not the spirit of personal selfishness, but a new spirit is going to come upon you. A holy spirit. Ye shall receive power, after that the Holy Spirit has come upon you. After that you are going to be possessed, saturated, captured, and motivated by a new spirit—a Holy spirit, a Godlike spirit."

And the nature of the power which will be yours is revealed in the nature of the spirit by which you are possessed because the spirit is the person. God is spirit. What kind of spirit? In Galatians 5: "The fruit of the Spirit is love." Love, joy, peace, long suffering, gentleness, goodness, faith, meekness, temperance. This is what God is like. This is what the Holy Spirit does in a person's life. These are the attributes the spirit of God creates in the person's living because this is God. These are the attributes of God, the attributes of the Spirit, the evidences of God's power. Love, joy, peace, long suffering, gentleness, goodness, and faith are what is to characterize a Christian, said Jesus. You're going to have a new spirit, and this new spirit is going to produce a new kind of person characterized by love. The Spirit will give you that, make you that, and produce that in you. It will multiply in your life like a tree flowers. It's going to grow. Now this spirit will be within a man, within any man, within every man who will open his heart to the grace of God. This new spirit not only creates a new kind of man motivated by different desires, but it creates an altogether new purpose for living. "Ye shall be my witnesses."

The word "witness" occurs 175 times in the New Testament, and interestingly enough there's only one word in the Greek language translated witness or martyr. A witness is a martyr. He is a man who no longer lives for himself. You can't tell this man you will take his life away because he's already given it away. He's no longer his own man. He's Christ's man. That's why the same word is translated witness and martyr. Because you see a witness is a martyr. He is a man who may be physically alive: "yet not I live but Christ lives in me," says Paul. He's motivated by an altogether different kind of spirit, so he's living for an altogether new kind of purpose. He is a witness. He does not witness as an act or to accumulate moral points, he is a witness. Witnessing is something he is. He goes through life characterized by love, and he is a witness. Not he does witnessing. He is a witness. Like a blind man who suddenly received his sight. A blind man who suddenly received his sight doesn't go around telling you all the time that he sees. You can tell by the way that he walks that he can see. You can tell by the way that he lives that he sees. Everything about his life is different because he now sees. He doesn't have to come up to you every day and say, "Look, I can see." You can see that he sees. Christ comes to give sight to the blind. He comes to let us see and seeing itself is a witness to the sight-giver, to Jesus Christ. When a man has been touched by this new power, filled with this new spirit, dedicated to this new purpose, his entire life will be reprogramed. He will be a witness where he is. He will begin in Jerusalem.

Why did they begin in Jerusalem? Because that's where they were. If they'd been in Galilee, Jesus would have said, "This is where you start. In Galilee, then to Jerusalem and all Judea, Samaria and to the uttermost part of the earth. You begin where you are."

Matthew 28 tells of the Great Commission. The eleven disciples went to the hill in Galilee where Jesus had told them to go, and when they saw him they worshiped him, even though some of them doubted. Jesus drew near and said to them, "I have been given all authority in heaven and on earth. Go then to all people everywhere and make them my disciples. Baptize them in the name of the Father, and of the Son, and of the Holy Spirit. Teach them to obey everything I have commanded you and remember I will be with you always to the end of the age." This is the basis of our going, our new program, our new purpose. We're to go.

And this word that Jesus speaks is an imperative. It is not an elective. Jesus is not saying go if you do not have anything better to do. He is not saying go if it is convenient and if it is approved by your family and friends. He is saying—you go.

There is a difference between the command of Jesus and the counsel of Jesus. "A new commandment I give you, love your enemies." That's a commandment. You don't have any choice there. But he said to one person, the rich young ruler, "Go sell everything you have and come to me." That's counseling. That is the application in life of the great principle and great command. He didn't tell every man to do that, but he did tell every man to love his enemies. That's a commandment. This is the new commandment. "Love them that hate you, and persecute you, and despitefully use you, and say all manner of evil against you falsely." Love them, that's a commandment. You go sell everything you have. Maybe that's not true for every man, but it is true for some.

You may know the Bible, you may be able to quote the Bible, you may memorize the Bible, know a lot of theology, but if you don't have the spirit of Christ, the scripture said, "If any man have not the spirit of Christ he's none of his." Go then, if you're God's man, if you're a spirit-motivated man, if you know Jesus Christ as Lord and Savior, it comes as an imperative to you to go.

Go where? Go right where you are in witnessing. An imperative. The literal translation of this passage is: As you are traveling about the world you are to make disciples. You do not have to go somewhere else to begin, but begin where you are, your home, your neighborhood, your school, right where you are, make disciples, witness.

What is your world? Well, my world today is not Africa,

South America or the Orient. My world today is where I live. Most of your world is where you live. When the Lord told us to go into all of the world, he was not speaking just geographically. Certainly we're to try to do that, but he was speaking not only extensively but intensively. He was saying, "Go into all of your world." Go into your personal world, business world, social world, church world, political world, economic world. You live in many worlds. Go into all of them, infiltrate them all. Witness in all of your world. You'll never get to all of the world geographically. You wouldn't have enough time to learn the languages, you wouldn't have enough time to saturate yourself with the culture so that your witness to those people would be effective. You're to go into all of your world— not somebody else's—yours. The world you live in, the world you rub shoulders with, the world you talk to. You already know the language. You don't have any language barrier, you don't have any cultural barrier, you're already there, you're already a part of it. Literally, as you travel about the world you're in, make disciples.

Now why do I need to do this? Why does Christ command me to do this? Because the Lord knows what you and I know when we stop to think about it. And that is that truth is not truth unless it is personified. A bell is no bell until you ring it, a song is no song till you sing it, and love is not put in your heart to stay for love is not love until you give it away.

This is why Jesus said, "I am the truth. Not I come to tell you the truth, but I am the truth. I am the light. I don't come to describe light for you, I come as light. I am the way. I don't come to show you the way or tell you where the way is, I am it." And truth must be personified to be truth. People occasionally say, "Well, what we need in the world is more honesty." I agree with that. What we need in the world is more truthfulness. Certainly I agree with that. What we need in the world today is peace. Surely, I'll agree with that. Anybody will. But listen, the only way for there to be more honesty in the world is for you and me to be more honest. The only way for there to be more truth in the world is for us to be more truthful. That's the only way truth has to get into life—to be there personified in me. The only way for there to be peace in the world is for me or for you to be a peacemaker. Truth does not exist in the abstract. Truth, to be truth, must be incarnated in flesh.

How do we give love away? We give it away by ministering, by witnessing to that which God loved, which is the world.

Dick Shepherd said, "Christianity consists, not in abstaining from doing things no gentleman would think of doing, but in doing things that are unlikely to occur to anyone who is not in touch with the Spirit of Christ." What in the world are we doing? What in the world are we doing, because Christ has done something in us?

Sam Shoemaker told the story in one of his books about a young Roman Catholic student in Paris who went to confession. He rather casually in a very offhand fashion confessed his sins without any indication of genuine penitence. The priest listened until the young man had finished and then because obviously he was a very wise priest said, "Young man, this is to be your penance. You know the location of Notre Dame cathedral?"

"Yes, Father."

"Then you're to go to the cathedral. Near the altar on the right hand side of the cathedral, there's a large crucifix mounted on the wall. You are to get down on your knees in front of that cross, and you are to say this in a loud voice so that you will hear yourself say it. You are to look at that symbolic representation of the death of Jesus and you are to say aloud 'Jesus, thou hast done this for me, but I don't give a damn.' "

"All right, Father."

So the boy went to the cathedral, got in front of the crucifix on his knees, and he said, "Jesus, thou hast done this for me. Jesus, thou hast done this for me." Finally out of the depths of his broken heart he cried, "Jesus, thou hast done this for me, and I care."

Do you care? If so, then what in the world are you doing for Christ's sake? What are you doing because you care?

14. The Christian Message of the Olympic Games

The first recorded Olympic games were held in 767 B.C. Just think of that—767 B.C. There are some historians who believe that the games were staged even hundreds of years earlier than that, but were not recorded. Greeks held the Olympic games on the Plain of Olympia in honor of Zeus, who was the king of the Greek gods. Gradually, all of the Greek city-states began to take part in the Olympics, sending a team from their city-state. In about 300 B.C., when the Greek states began to decline and disintegrate, other nations began to send participants to the Olympic games. Then about A.D. 394 the Olympic games ceased. Fifteen hundred years passed, and in 1896, there was a reorganization of the Olympics in Athens, and the rest is modern history. Something else, the Isthmian games were held in Corinth, and these games were celebrated every two years. And in these games, no one but Greeks of pure blood who had done nothing to forfeit their citizenship were allowed to participate. These were the greatest of national gatherings, and even when one state was at war with another state, hostilities were suspended for the celebration of the games.

Apparently the apostle Paul was a frequent spectator, if not possibly even a participant, at one time in his life, in these great games. He draws so many analogies from the athletic events of his day. But we are certain of his enthusiasm for and in all probability, his participation in athletics. He writes to the folks in Corinth, where the Isthmian games were held every two years. "You know that in a race, all the runners take part, but only one of them wins the prize."

Every athlete in training submits to strict discipline. He does so in order to be crowned with a wreath that will not last, but we run our race for One that will last forever. Run straight for the finish line. Be like a boxer who does not waste his punches.

"That I might win," is not only the dominating, compelling theme of Paul's life, but it is the high music of his entire life. This is Paul's deepest prayer, his passion, his purpose, the driving power of his whole life, "That I might win." No language is too strong to describe it. Every tributary of his own personality flowed into this one main stream until it had the force of a raging torrent. Paul recognized that which the New Testament so clearly teaches, and which life confirms. For a man to win he must participate. There's nothing profound about that statement, and yet so many of us expect in this business of Christian living to win without participation.

"Every Christian is in this race," that's what Paul said. Everybody's running, everybody's in it. The only people who are allowed to be spectators are those individuals who have already gone on to be with the Lord, and even they are more than spectators. They are spectators who interpret to us the meaning of our race, the meaning of our struggle, and who bear testimony to the certainty of our triumph if we continue steadfastly, persistently in the race. Their example, and their presence is meant to stimulate us. They applaud for us. Run! Go! Stay with it!

There are no spectators in the life of the church. None. The nature of salvation, the meaning of membership in a body, precludes the possibility of being an onlooker. It is impossible. The very nature of salvation precludes it. The very nomenclature used to describe our salvation precludes it. It is impossible to be a Christian and to be a spectator at the same time.

There is a crippling feeling abroad in the land today. Let the professionals do it. That's what we pay them to do. We will be passive onlookers, we will watch from the safety of the grandstands. My, we see that it is not only in the area of the church, not only in the area of Christian discipleship, we see it in so many areas. And we see it in our national life in the area of politics. You know the background of the word idiot, the Greek word that gave rise to the English word translated idiot? It means a person who will not participate in the affairs of life. That's what an idiot is. A person who doesn't participate.

We are all ministers of Christ—all of us. I happen, as part of my ministry of Christ to be pastor of Trinity Baptist Church, but all of us are ministers. Ministers for Christ. Now we do not all participate in the same event. We're not all pastors. We're not all teachers. We're not all apostles or prophets, but we're all members of the team. Somebody runs the 100 yard dash, somebody else runs the 880, but they're still members of the same team. To use another analogy, we're not all quarterbacks, we're not all ends, we're not all tackles, we're not all guards, but we're all on the team. The proper terminology for what the church staff does is that of player-coach. We're in the game, but we're also there to try to direct it, but we're all on the team. No spectators. My, the New Testament emphasizes this over and over again. Paul saw it, he underlines it for us, you are on the team.

In the light of this, you must determine your goal. Paul inevitably found himself tempted from time to time to rest in the name and the calling of an apostle, to take for granted that since his salvation was settled, there need be no more thought, no more effort, no more work expended. And he saw that in a slightly altered form, this temptation came to all Christians. You see, all have the name, but not all have the reality. And the very possession of the name, Christian, is a temptation to take for granted or even to forget the reality which must be present behind that name. Paul recognized that he was not saved by proclaiming the gospel to others any more than the baker is fed merely because he makes bread for others, or any more than the physician stays healthy by simply prescribing help for others. It must be a fact, a power, a presence in his own life.

Paul had to lead his own life. He had his own duty to perform, his own responsibility to discharge, and he recognized that what was laid before him as the path of salvation was to make himself as a servant for others. And exactly the same thing is true for us. "The greatest among you" said Jesus, "will be the servant of all." So the concern of the Christian, the object of the Christian, is not to get out of the race, but to get in it, not to get to a place where he can relax, but to get to a place where he can expend more of himself. To build up his spiritual reserves, his spiritual stamina, so that his life can be characterized, not by relaxation, but by enthusiastic, effervescent, effective participation. We've got it backwards, many of us. And in an endeavor to warn Christians against resting in a mere profession of faith in Christ, Paul draws an example from these world renowned Olympic games. "All run," he said, "but one receiveth the prize." Now, Paul does not mean that salvation goes by competition. That's not what he's talking about at all. But he means that in a race, a physical race, not all who run, run so as to obtain the prize. So in the Christian life.

Not all who enter put out sufficient energy to bring him a spiritual gold medal. The mere fact of recognizing that the prize is worth winning and even desiring to have it is not enough. You must run, Paul says. You can want it, you can desire it, you can say it's worth having, but you've got to participate to get it. You must run. You must be a member of this spiritual Olympic team. You must be in training. Now you are on the team, you are determining your goal. This passage teaches us that to be victorious in this race demands discipline. One must be willing to pay the price. Now admittedly this is not easy. The Lord did not promise that it would be easy. He said, "If any man will come after me let him deny himself, take up his cross daily, and follow me."

We try to find shortcuts, and try to get around it, but it just does not work. We know that nothing worth having is ever realized easily. Nothing. Christian character is not made in a few spare moments on a rainy Sunday morning. It is important to go to church, the gymnasium of faith, but the building of strength and Christian character, like the building of the physique of an athlete, requires daily workouts, daily participation, daily training. Robert Browning said, "When the fight begins within himself, a man's worth something."

Man and steel are alike in that both are uncertain until they have been fired and until they have been tested. You and I will never be effective for Christ as his disciples until we accept daily discipline and dedication in our Christian race. We need to discipline our bodies. It is one of the neglected facts of the spiritual life that very often, very often the spiritual depression springs from nothing else but physical unfitness. I've seen it happen. I've seen it happen to myself. If a man is going to do his best work in anything, he must bring to it a body as fit as he can make it. We neglect our physical health at our peril. If the body is the temple of the Holy Spirit, as we Christian believe because the Bible teaches it, then we have a divine responsibility to take care of our bodies and to give to God the best possible body that good habits, good practices, and good exercise can provide. To do otherwise is a sin against God.

Also we must discipline our minds. It is one of the tragedies of life that men refuse to think until they are incapable of thinking. We never solve problems by refusing to see them, we never solve problems by running away from them.

One way for the discipline of souls is through temperance. A flabby, overweight athlete, short of breath, may run, but he's not going to win any races. And an overweight, slack, lazy, indifferent, casual Christian may get to heaven, but he won't win the race that's set before him here. Paul says that we must regard ourselves as men who are on a campaign, as athletes who are in training, as individuals who are pressing on toward a tremendous goal. We must apply the same stringent training rules to our souls that an athlete applies to his body to win the Olympic games. For the contest in which the Christian is engaged is not any less severe, but rather it is even more severe than an athletic contest. And the temperance maintained by the athlete must be outdone by the Christian if he is to be successful as a member of God's team.

This spiritual training, like physical training, to be effective, must be complete. An athlete must develop his entire body, all of his muscles, not just a few muscles. Likewise the Christian must have his entire life involved in the cause of Christ. He simply cannot segregate his business life from his spiritual life, his home life from his spiritual life, his social life from his spiritual life. To train only a certain set of spiritual muscles, to train only the spiritual muscles that will be operating on Sunday morning at 8:15 or 11:00 o'clock is to court disaster, and you'll never win in this race.

The spiritual athlete, like the physical athlete, in his training, must be continuous. A man must stay with it. I guess maybe it's happened to all of us at one time or another. We started out so well, got revived at a revival meeting or some circumstance came in our life that we rightly interpreted as God's way of saying, "Get in the race." We started. My, we were so enthusiastic for a while, we read our Bibles and prayed. We were ready to visit and talk to people about Christ and to go to church and to be there. And then the weather got bad or we got tired and we just fizzled out. We looked great the first 100 yards. We maybe made it around the track one time, but by then we were finding that it wasn't as easy as it looked. Instead of paying the price necessary to maintain or to increase spiritual conditioning, we quit. Now, I understand this because it's happened to me, maybe it's happened to you. One reason we do get discouraged is because it looks so much easier when we start. We get tired pretty quickly, and so we quit. Instead of staying with it so that our stamina increases we pull back.

I want to use a personal example. Three years ago I said to my friend, Dr. Kenneth Cooper, who is an active member of our church and is recognized by many as the outstanding authority of the world on physical fitness, "I get kind of tired, 41 years old this next month, I'm not satisfied with my physical conditioning. I mean, if I walk a little bit maybe I can kind of get back into shape." I envisioned myself as being in pretty good physical condition, participated in athletics, played golf occasionally.

He said, "Well, let me give you this test. The way you find

whether or not you're in good shape is to see if you can run a mile-and-a-half in twelve minutes."

I said, "That's kinda easy." I'm sure Dr. Cooper was rather amused by my attitude, but I felt like I could do *that!* You've never seen such a fizzle in your life. You think that sounds easy, you try it this afternoon! I barely made a little over a mile in twelve minutes. That was three years ago; now I can run three miles, averaging about seven-and-a-half or eight-and-a-half minutes a mile. I never felt better in my life.

The point I want to make is that everything looks easier before you start, but there's nothing in the world as exciting as getting with it, participating.

The same thing will happen in your Christian life. You'll begin and you'll think, "My goodness, this thing's so easy looking at it from a distance. Why anybody can do that." But anybody can't do that. And temptation comes, and you didn't think it was going to be there. You thought you had more reserves than you have, and you thought you had more internal strength than you have. You thought you had more power than you have, but that recognition, rather than discouraging you, ought to inspire you to pay the price necessary to run with persistence the race that's set before you. What you and I need is motivation for physical exercise, for mental exercise, and for spiritual exercise. What we need is something of the sense of the reality of the life and death struggle we are engaged in. A lot of us are not serious about what we're talking about. We need to be reminded that the man who treats the Christian commitment casually or with a sense of indifference or with spasmodic, occasional training will shortly be dragged in mangled disgrace out of the arena of life.

We need a sense of the seriousness of this cause in which we are engaged because we're going to win. We are going to stay with it, we are going to train, we are going to practice, we are going to work, we are going to make the sacrifices necessary to do it. We are going to win. Paul declared in the closing hours of his life, "I fought a good fight. I have finished my course." There are those two analogies; he uses them again right here at the close of his life. "I've fought a good fight, I have finished the race, I kept the faith, henceforth, there is laid up for me a crown. I won it. A crown of righteousness which the Lord, the righteous Judge, shall give to me at that day, but not to me only, but also unto all them that paid the price, that love his appearance." We are going to be more than conquerors through Jesus Christ our Lord, and we're going to win. We are going to win because our Lord has set the example and has given us the incentive. We're going to do it.

Many of you will remember Glen Cunningham. The fantastic, remarkable story of a boy, who at eight years of age was so badly burned that the doctors told him he would never walk again. A schoolhouse explosion and fire killed his brother and burned him badly. He said, "I was miserable at the thought of being an invalid all my life, and I might have been had I not had a Mother who was filled with such great hope and faith that she wouldn't let me give up."

"She'd say, 'The Lord made you whole, and he wants you whole now.' She told me time and time again. 'You'll not only walk, Glen, you will run, you'll play. I believe it, and you believe it, and it will happen.' "

To a child, a Mother's words are divine. "She poured her hope and her faith in me, but she did more than talk. For hours each day until her arms were numb, she massaged my lifeless legs. When she had to stop for supper or other household work, she had me do the massaging. 'Keep working at it, son.' "

"And I did. Six months later I was walking. In a few more

months, I was able to trot just a little. Soon a limp was the only trace of the accident. And at age twelve, I ran and won a schoolboy race. When I got home, Mother smiled, but she didn't think of it as the end of anything. 'Just keep working at it, son. Keep working at it. You can do anything you set your heart to do.' " Many of you know what happened. Glen Cunningham went on to set the world outdoor mark in 1934, the world indoor mark in 1938, and ran on the United States Olympic Team. Today he runs a ranch for delinquent boys and girls in Kansas.

Do you know why? First of all because he had somebody care. That was the incentive, that was the motive behind it. He had faith, he had a challenge, and he had a goal. He paid the price, and he stayed with it. He completed the task, he won.

Now I want to be a winner. You want to win. You want to be the best possible individual that your native equipment refined to its highest and best will allow you to be, don't you? Well, you can be. Stay with it, son. Start, train, pay the price, and you'll make it. You'll be more than conqueror through Jesus Christ our Lord. Run with perseverance the race that's set before you.

Let Christ get into your shoes, and you will be a winner in the race of life.